DRIVEN GAME
SHOOTING

DRIVEN GAME SHOOTING

DEREK BINGHAM

Photographs by

ALASTAIR DREW

UNWIN

HYMAN

LONDON SYDNEY WELLINGTON

First published in Great Britain by the Trade Division of Unwin Hyman Ltd,
15–17 Broadwick Street, London W1V 1FP
Allen & Unwin Pty Ltd, 8 Napier Street, North Sydney, NSW 2060, Australia
Allen & Unwin New Zealand Pty Ltd, with Port Nicholson Press
Compusales Building, 75 Ghuznee Street, Wellington, New Zealand

© This edition Antler Books Ltd 1989

Produced by John Stidolph
Designed by Humphrey Stone
Paintings and drawings by Andrew Stock

British Library Cataloguing in Publication Data
Bingham, Derek
Driven game shooting.
1. Great Britain.   Game birds.   Shooting – Amateurs' manuals
I. Title
799.2′4′0941

ISBN 0-04-440418-2

Published simultaneously with the Trade Hardback Edition
are three signed, limited and specially bound editions,
available from The Marlborough Bookshop & Sporting Gallery,
6 Kingsbury Street, Marlborough, Wiltshire
Full leather, limited to 50 copies, with an original watercolour sketch
ISBN 0-04-4405952
Full leather, limited to 100 copies, with pencil/ink remarque
ISBN 0-04-4405960
Quarter leather, limited to 200 copies
ISBN 0-04-4405979

Typeset by Ace Filmsetting, Frome, Somerset
Originated by BBE Colour Ltd
Printed by Graficomo SA, Cordoba, Spain

Contents

Author's Acknowledgements

Warm thanks go to many people who have helped with this book, and in particular to Richard and Lavinia Beaumont, Nigel Beaumont and Lawrie Salter of James Purdey and Sons Ltd for their help with the chapters on gunmaking, accessories and clothing; to the British Association for Shooting and Conservation; to Nigel Brown, secretary of the Gun Trade Association, for his help with guns and the law; to Peter Denny for his help with the gundog chapters; to Graham Downing of the Country Landowners' Association; to Keith and Jean Howman of the World Pheasant Association for help with game birds; to Dr Mike Swan and the Game Conservancy; to Pim and Peter Veenbaas on whose shoot I have spent many happy days; and to David Wright, the Guildford ear specialist, for advice on the damage shooting can do to hearing.

A sincere thank you, too, to Alastair Drew for his hard work with the camera, to John Stidolph and Merlin Unwin for their support and encouragement, and to Vicki and the girls for putting up with it all.

DEREK BINGHAM
Easton, 1989

Andrew Stock 82 ©

The Artist and the Paintings

THE ARTIST

Andrew Stock was born in 1960 in Germany, where his father was serving with the Royal Artillery. In his last year at Sherborne he had an interview with Sir Peter Scott which resulted in his becoming a professional artist as soon as he left school.

He has been fascinated by birds all his life, has watched them closely, and by his mid teens was drawing and painting them with considerable skill. He has had no further tuition since leaving school, but his bird paintings have been widely acclaimed.

In 1980 he won the Richard Richardson Award for bird illustration. In 1981 he had the first of his one-man exhibitions at the prestigious Malcolm Innes Gallery; and in 1983 he was elected one of the youngest members of the Society of Wildlife Artists. Further one-man exhibitions followed in 1983, 1987 and 1989.

Andrew Stock is married and in 1984 moved back to West Dorset to a countryside which he feels is ideal for a practising bird artist.

THE PAINTINGS

When I was asked to illustrate this book I decided that I wished to present the birds as I had seen and studied them, rather than in the classic sporting print style of old. I also decided to show them in the plumage of the shooting season, as that is how they would be best known to most of the readers.

Two of the plates merit particular comment; first, Woodcock, which I have shown in boggy ground, feeding; in fact just behind my house. I prefer to show them that way rather than resting among leaves. Second, Grouse, which are shown as I see them on my regular visits to Sutherland where the ground is boggy, and coarse grass vies with the heather over much of the moor.

ANDREW STOCK

THE DRIVEN DAY

Dramatis personae of a driven game shoot: Host and head gamekeeper line up with Guns and other guests, catering staff, beaters, pickers-up and stops.

PICTURE the scene. It is 9.15 on a bright November morning, a nip in the air and the sun emphasising the autumn russet as you drive through the gates. You have been invited for a day's driven game shooting, and the party is already assembling in front of the mellow country house.

If you are new to shooting you may, as you approach, suffer by no means your first but probably your most acute attack of nerves. All sorts of doubts will begin to appear. Will you shoot straight? Are your stripy socks too gaudy? (probably not). Will you look out of place in protective ear muffs? (no). Will your host mind that you have brought your other half along? (possibly, but he will be much too polite to say so). Will he mind if you take your portable telephone so that your office can ring you? (most probably, and you may find that even his politeness has limits).

Meanwhile Guns greet the host, and their gundogs circle each other warily. To one side stand the beaters, and on another the pickers-up, their dogs waiting patiently. The conversation is cheerful, reflecting the anticipation of the day's sport to come as well as helping to mask any nerves among the Guns. Host and his head 'keeper move from group to group, ensuring that all is well. Numbers are drawn and the host gives instructions. 'Guns this way please' comes the order.

It all looks very complicated, very organised; it is very expensive, and you are unsure of your place in it. A seasoned Gun takes it all in his stride, experience enabling him to cope with the conventions of dress and etiquette in a sport bound by unwritten rules, and the confidence to shoot straight.

You will learn from experience too, and in the meantime we can provide you with the more important tips. But as you move off you can rest assured that, if you have done your homework, everything will fall into place. The most important thing is not to worry. You are here to enjoy yourself, and if you set out to do that, you will.

In Britain driven shooting means the driving of live quarry to a line of standing Guns. Peter Dorhout Mees in action as pheasants cross the line at Sledmere in North Yorkshire. The labrador marks a fallen bird.

Driven Game

Driven shooting in Britain means the driving of live quarry, usually game birds and ground game or wildfowl, to a line of standing Guns. It differs from walking up, in which Guns walk in a line through cover with dogs to flush the game; from flighting pigeon or duck, in which the Gun awaits the quarry as they fly in to feed or roost; wildfowling, which is the pursuit of wildfowl on the foreshore; and clay pigeon shooting, a competitive branch of the sport using artificial targets launched from a trap.

Although driven shooting is one of the most recent forms of the sport, it is the most formal, expensive, socially conscious and highly organised. It will involve factors as diverse as law, farming, forestry, aviculture, ballistics, dog handling, topography, technology, natural history, weather, fashion, finance, insurance, socialising, ethics, and man management. And although to some people it might seem an anachronism in the 1990s, to others it is part of an enduring rural scene with its roots firmly established in history.

Since Norman times countless country houses have witnessed the sight of parties meeting to hunt boar, deer or fox, course hares, or fly falcons to game and wildfowl. The driven game shoot, and a meet of hounds, are the modern form of this tradition. Times and circumstances may change but the role of field sports (or country sports as they are called) in the countryside remains as important as ever. It could be said that they fulfilled two important roles in the last two centuries, whether intentional or not. They helped to keep landowners on their land, managing it, and not absent in the bright lights of the city. They also provided a regular channel for communication in the countryside. It is even argued that in doing so they helped to keep Britain relatively stable in the last two centuries – certainly while much of Europe has seen violent revolution Britain has not. Whether this is true or not, country sports are firmly entrenched in our natural heritage. More important, they are now more popular than ever and have a significant role for recreation, employment, the rural economy, and conservation.

More than 80% of the population now lives in towns, but wants to use the countryside for recreation. Thanks to an idyllic rural image (which has never existed) created by television advertisements and fostered by some conservationists, it is not surprising that few people appreciate the complexities of modern land management. Modern country sports provide not only badly-needed recreational opportunities, but a way to channel newcomers into the countryside which allows them to absorb their surroundings gradually and, in time, to understand what is at stake.

Britain's green and pleasant land, and remaining heather moorlands and marshes

A Gun awaits the grouse: Were it not for grouse-shooting more heather moorlands, and the diverse wildlife they support, would disappear.

for that matter, are not still there by accident. Farming pressures have been with us for centuries and the fact that we have so much good shooting, fishing and hunting and diversity of wildlife which is the envy of many other countries, has happened because people wanted it that way and over the centuries were prepared to do something about it. That required more than the specific knowledge to preserve and manage game and wildlife. It also needed political, legal and social frameworks which accepted them. Words and phrases in the English language and Parliamentary terms and expressions (Whips in the Houses of Parliament come from 'whippers-in' on the hunting field), derive directly from our traditional country sports.

In addition to preserving the woodlands and marshes, and planting and managing coverts for the benefit of other wildlife as well as gamebirds and deer, country sports

On a fine November day Peter Duckworth, watched by his neice, Dr Katherine Acland, awaits a pheasant from Searchlight Wood on Lord Clitheroe's Downham estate.

act as a brake on modern farming excesses. They are in a unique position to monitor what happens in the countryside – it was the shooting fraternity which first warned of the effects of chemicals on wildlife, just in the same way that it has been the anglers who have been at the forefront of campaigning to keep our rivers clean. In addition an increasing amount of valuable scientific information is becoming available as a direct result of research instigated by field sports. They generate enormous sums of money in the rural economy. A survey undertaken at the beginning of the 1980s by Cobham Resource Consultants for the Standing Conference on Countryside Sports put the figure at nearly £2 billion a year, with obvious implications for employment, from gunmaking to running a hotel, which Cobham put at nearly 90,000 jobs.

Sports also have implications for the price of land. The creation of a shoot adds to the capital value of an estate and provides a source of income. Shoot rentals may increase revenue by £3 an acre per annum. A wood may provide £100 an acre income as game cover in addition to the value of the timber. There are generous grants available for planting coverts, and excellent scientific advice.

So the day you are about to enjoy is even more complex than might at first appear, but you can find out about the background as time goes by. In the meantime you will have more than enough on your plate to play your own part. It may all seem a bit daunting if you are new to the sport, but the answers are relatively simple providing you recognise the priorities.

It is best to concentrate initially on three priorities. One is your obligation in law, without which you cannot venture out to shoot. The second is your obligation to the quarry. That means learning how to shoot, and not shooting at live quarry until you are sufficiently accurate. The third obligation is to your host, fellow sportsmen and others who share the shooting field with you. The rest will fall into place as you go along and gain confidence. And above all remember that you are there to enjoy yourself.

A HISTORY LESSON

THE popularity of modern shooting is extraordinary if you consider that compared with coursing, falconry or hunting with hounds the sport is still in its infancy. Whatever the reasons for this, shooting is the one sport (although arguably fishing must also be considered in this context) which has depended on our ability to develop and master technology rather than to rely on training animals to help us hunt, although they still play an important part in the process. Even if the development of this technology, in the form of gunmaking and mastery of ballistics, was for war rather than sport, it is a sign of man's ingenuity that he was able to adapt it for other purposes.

Nevertheless the foundations of modern driven game shooting were laid, and the guns used were being perfected, before the car was invented, women had the vote, or the British cavalry had charged in anger for the last time. The whole process took less than half a century, a fraction of the time it took for the arts of coursing and falconry to permeate from the East.

Olden Days

It was also from the Far East that gunpowder, with its implications for war, probably came. From the time of its arrival in the West, and the development of the first guns simultaneously in several parts of Europe in the thirteenth and fourteenth centuries, it was not until the Stuart era that two things occurred to enhance their use for sporting purposes.

The first was that guns became accepted in the sporting field. Perhaps the only surprise is that it took such a short time. If one considers how old the traditions of hunting with hound, hawk, spear and arrow were even at that time, resistance to the new-fangled, noisy, smelly and dangerous gun was not surprising. Signs of that resistance still exist, and opinions in the sporting world are as hard held now as they probably were then.

Even before Stuart times guns were used on birds and deer for food; their use in wars ensured that there were sufficient numbers around and that on occasions they were used for non-warlike uses. But the sporting ethic in Britain was more conservative than those of other European countries (it still is), and it became longer for the new method of killing game to be accepted as 'sporting'.

The second development was that the design and manufacture of guns had advanced to make them both sufficiently stable and efficient for use on the sporting field. The most significant development was that of the wheel lock in the sixteenth century, in turn leading to the snaplock and the flintlock, which was to provide the instantaneous ignition essential for successfully shooting live quarry. To these developments were added advances in metals, ballistics and craftsmanship. The flintlock became one of the finest examples of the gunmaker's art.

Two major developments in the nineteenth century laid the foundations of modern driven game shooting. One was the introduction of the percussion system of ignition, and the other the breech-loader. They had a major influence on both the safety of guns and, significantly, on the speed with which they could be reloaded.

It was at the Great Exhibition at Crystal Palace in 1851 that Lefaucheux's pin-fire breechloading shotgun, from which the modern shotgun has developed in Britain, was first seen. In the 1870s the hammerless boxlock gun began to supercede the hammergun; the ejector system and the more elegant sidelock followed shortly after. Since then there have been refinements and improvements, but the basic design and mechanism of both the sidelock and boxlock favoured by game shots have remained unaltered.

One of the effects of our political system down the ages has been the localising of power and the fact that landowners tended to stay on their land. This in turn led to the development of 'local' distractions to provide enjoyment, and is the main reason why field sports are so deeply embedded in our traditions.

Thus an impetus behind the developments in gunmaking was provided by the growing interest in sporting shooting, and each development had its effects on the sport. Even before the percussion system shooting was an established rural pastime, as the old sporting prints show. Mostly it was a leisurely affair, sometimes solitary, behind pointers at birds which were inevitably flying away. In this type of shooting the speed of reloading was not important. Once the covey of partridges, the pheasant or the wildfowl had been flushed and the gun fired, there was no further action until the dog was instructed to continue the search for quarry. Though it was more efficient than the flintlock, and made reloading easier, the percussion cap made no material difference to the pace of sport.

Killing large numbers of birds, or shooting at them flying towards the Gun, were not even considered until, in the mid-nineteenth century, the principle of the *battue*

PREVIOUS PAGE *In the face of intensive farming and other pressures, Britain's green and pleasant land is not still there by accident. Sir Tatton Sykes's Schoolhouse Dale at Sledmere may owe its shape to ancient glaciers, but it has been planted and nurtured to make the most of natural features to show high birds.*

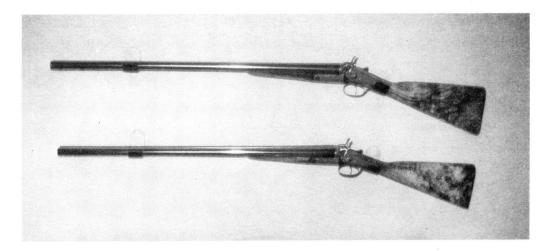

This pair of Purdey 12-bore hammer guns was built for Lord Ripon, one of the finest game shots of all time, more than 100 years ago.

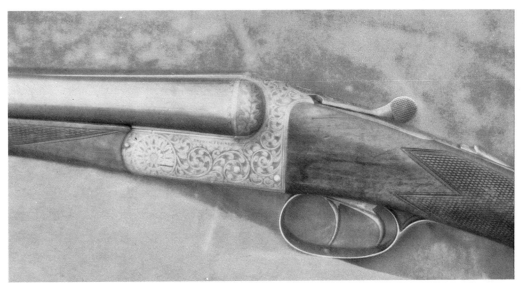

An English 12-bore boxlock: Tough, reliable, and less expensive than a sidelock.

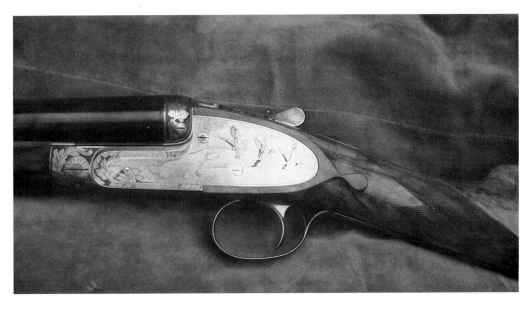

A Purdey single-trigger 12-bore sidelock, with engraving, costs in the region of £20,000. The elegant sidelock was perfected in the last century.

was adapted to shooting birds and the development of the breech-loading gun made fast reloading possible, the one encouraging the development of the other.

Battue was an old French term for driving large numbers of animals towards hunters. The aim was to kill as many of the former as possible. The skill of the chase, which in Britain had long been the main challenge and enjoyment of the hunt, came secondary to the ability to kill. The fact that the word has also crept into the English language suggests that the practice was not unknown on English estates with deer parks where large quantities of venison were sometimes needed.

But the implications for sporting shooting were far-reaching. It is not difficult to imagine conflicting philosophies of those used to pursuing their sport alone, in harmony with nature and having to work hard for success, and those who preferred the more active, artificial and competitive *battue* with its growing social overtones. These attitudes are evident today in the way the various branches of shooting – driven, rough, stalking, wildfowling and clay pigeon – have developed independently of each other.

Golden Days

However, driven game shooting might not have developed had it not been for circumstances in the latter part of the nineteenth century which had little to do with either guns or game.

From 1861, when Queen Victoria withdrew after the death of Prince Albert, the Prince and Princess of Wales assumed the leadership of society. The interest in, not to say passion for, the sport shown by the Prince of Wales, later King Edward VII, coincided with the era of the fruits of the industrial revolution. Large wealth, and royal direction, proved a potent combination. The lead given by the Prince's purchase of Sandringham in Norfolk before his wedding to Princess Alexandra in 1864, and his development of driven game shooting there (he even experimented with the introduction of red grouse and Virginia quail), was followed by numerous other estates.

Big estates dominated and controlled life in the countryside. There were staff, land and money. In addition to the aristocracy and gentry there were aspiring *nouveaux riches*, who added elements of ostentation and competition. The new railways revolutionised transport, allowing sportsmen to expand their horizons in safety, comfort and convenience and enjoy, for instance, the superb sporting fare in Scotland as well as the shooting parties nearer home.

It was the era when up to four guns were used by each Gun, when shooting parties continued for four days, and the lunches were as sparkling as the company. It was the era of the record bag of nearly 4000 pheasants shot in a day at Hall Barn,

Baron von Tuyll, Mr Andriessen and some very high pheasants indeed.

Buckinghamshire; of Lord Ripon, who on one occasion was credited with shooting 28 pheasants in a minute and on another is claimed to have had seven dead birds in the air at once. In 56 years shooting he personally accounted for more than half a million head. It was the era of the sixth Lord Walsingham who in one day in 1888 shot 1070 grouse on Blubberhouse Moor, Yorkshire and who was to be made bankrupt by shooting; of Sir Ralph Payne Gallwey, great shot, eccentric, whose books on shooting remain classics; and of Sir Frederick Milbank who shot 190 grouse in one drive at Wemmergill, Yorkshire in 1872.

The Edwardian shooting party became a highly stylised version of the sport, a reflection of an era, and it bequeathed two legacies to shooting. One is that, ever since, driven game shooting has fought to shrug off the taint of excess.

The second was more constructive. Large bags required the development of shoot management. Most of the techniques used today of siting and planting of coverts, rearing and releasing birds, beating coverts and the development of gundog work have their foundations in the last century. As well as Sandringham, the methods used at Elveden, Holkham and Euston and a host of other great estates have all left their mark.

Shooting on such a grand scale, a scale which is unacceptable nowadays, disappeared with the First World War. The austerity of the post-war years had the

'Ignoring the bird that flies too low': Nicholas van Cutsem makes the right decision.

'. . . or too high': On the Range Drive at Richard Clarke's Chilcomb Shoot near Winchester in Hampshire, this bird is on the border line.

effect both of refining and redefining. Although these were difficult times for estates, farming and the countryside, they are often regarded as something of a golden era for field sports. There were no farming pressures to affect game or wildlife adversely, or to impede the progress of hounds and hunt across the countryside. Because estates had to make do with what they had in the way of manpower, they used it wisely. Social attitudes and money still had a restricting influence on the numbers who went hunting or shooting, and opposition to field sports was mute.

In shooting the sporting ethic re-asserted itself over the needs for large bags or competitive shooting. From this re-assertion came the emphasis on the 'sporting bird' and the quality of shooting rather than the quantity. Not that the ethic had necessarily disappeared, but on some shoots it may have become submerged. After all, for the large bags to have been shot and legendary reputations created suggests a certain crowding of the airways. From now on the fewer birds that did come forward would be 'sporting'. And the aim of the Guns was to account only for the sporting bird – one which has as much chance of escaping as the Gun has of killing it cleanly – while ignoring those which flew too low or, for that matter, too high.

Modern Days

It is from these foundations that modern driven game shooting has developed, but the world in which it now takes place has changed out of all recognition. The era of car, plane, and instant communication would have been as inconceivable to our Victorian forbears as the freedom we have to pick and choose our recreations and the time and money to pursue them.

Most people now live in towns and cities. Their need for recreation and for contact with the countryside has introduced a new generation to shooting which includes many who have no rural background. At the same time modern conditions and expertise have allowed the shooting enthusiast to become involved in the wider aspects of the sport, with the result that there is a far greater awareness of the sporting ethic and ability to put it into practice in shoot management.

However since the Second World War have come intensive farming, development and mobility, all putting pressures on a dwindling amount of countryside. So in addition to providing recreation, shooting must involve itself with conservation, act as buffer and watchdog against farming excesses, and help educate people about the countryside and wildlife.

There are also some similarities with a century ago. Since then the country has never been as economically sound as it is now. There are time, money, and new attitudes in abundance. However although the influx of money into shooting in the

The grouse remains the supreme sporting bird, and this scene of the pick-up after the famous Hook drive on Haredon Fell in the Trough of Bowland represents the culmination of much skill, hard work and splendid shooting.

last decade has been generally beneficial, some less than welcome echoes from an earlier era have reappeared. The main one is increasing evidence of the unhealthy tendency to judge the success of a day on the size of the bag. Even more unhealthy for the sport's image is the way in which birds are produced to shoot. The modern packaging and marketing of shooting has become sophisticated in response to a demand, mainly from business, for entertainment. On the fringes of this are the unscrupulous to whom the sporting ethic is an obstacle to profit, and where the degree of entertainment is measured by an easy killing. At a sensitive time when all field sports are matter of public debate, shooting can do without this sort of thing.

There is sufficient concern about what is going on for the three main bodies involved with shooting – the British Association for Shooting and Conservation, Game Conservancy and British Field Sports Society – to start preparing guidelines for the management of shoots.

Andrew Stock 89 ©

RIGHTS AND VALUES

THE Victorian era established driven game shooting as a source of recreation, employment, rural finance and conservation. These factors are also relevant now. Furthermore shooting has become more popular and farming's influence on the rural economy and as an employer has also changed. Whether foxhunters accept it or not, shooting has now superceded it as the most influential country sport. This is both because more people actively participate in it and because of its ability to attract money to the countryside. This can be seen both in terms of direct and indirect employment, and in the rental and capital values of land.

Since Norman times game rights have been recognised in law. As well as providing a legal framework for the hunting and preservation of game species, it also means that certain types of shooting and fishing rights are negotiable assets. These rights can be separated from the ownership of the land or water over which they take place. Those who shoot, but do not own the shooting rights, must therefore expect to have to pay for the privilege of enjoying them as well as the cost of producing the quarry.

This legal framework does not extend to hunting fox or hare with hounds (foxes are regarded as vermin), which takes place over land by consent of the landowners. Hence no fee is paid and, unlike shooting, the sport provides the landowner with no financial benefit.

The values attached to sporting rights apply mainly to the game birds (pheasants, partridges, grouse, blackgame and ptarmigan) and fish (salmon, trout, sea trout, greyling) and deer which, according to a recent court ruling, are not game in England and Wales. Their values to the owner of the sporting rights, in terms of rental or capital, vary according to supply and demand, situation, quality of management, and on whether the quarry is wild (grouse, deer, or salmon for instance) or reared and released especially for sporting purposes. Capital or rental values are expressed either in £ per acre or as the value per head killed. An estate's sporting potential can be gauged by its game records over the years. The more accurate they are the better the chance of achieving a fair value for the sporting rights.

Britain is exceptionally lucky in that it has the climate and conditions suitable for a large variety of resident and migrant birds, animals and fish which, by and large, have been better managed over the centuries than in many other countries. In addition the expertise is also now available to maximise sporting potential without adversely affecting quarry populations, and also to create shoots and fisheries from scratch. But the effect sporting values have on their surroundings varies according to other land uses.

The bag can make a valuable contribution to a shoot's economy. Here young hands help to sort and hang partridges at Sutton Scotney in Hampshire.

Highland

In the Scottish uplands for instance, where the only other sources of income from the land may be forestry or hill farming (and in places even they may not be possible), shooting, stalking or fishing have a major economic significance. The fact that all the quarry are the wild species (except for some reared pheasants and partridges) also adds enormously to the sporting value. Grouse, red deer, salmon and sea trout attract sportsmen from all over the world, and for top-quality sport demand exceeds supply.

Since the war their values have increased steadily. Within the last five years they have doubled in some instances, and demand for sporting estates which harbour them has been exceptionally strong. In part this has been due to demand created by a strong British economy being added to the existing demand from abroad. There has been a need to find new areas for investing money made in the City. Although this source of funds was expected to diminish after Big Bang 1986, it continued and increased.

Strutt and Parker, the estate agents who sold the Glenmoriston estate on the shores of Loch Ness (10,000 acres of deer forest, grouse moors, forestry and salmon fishing, asking price £3.5 million) in 1988, reported that instead of the usual score of enquiries they had to send out some 3000 brochures to potential buyers in this country, America, Europe and Hong Kong. The estate was sold for more than the asking price. One agent specialising in grouse moors says that he has so much money waiting in the wings from potential purchasers that if a good estate does come on the market its value will be artificially inflated. Another says that the fact that large tracts of wild land are increasingly difficult to buy in Europe has added a further premium to the sporting value of Scottish estates.

The capital value of a deer forest is currently quoted at up to £15,000 per stag,

Grouse are the most valuable game birds: Sportsmen must expect to pay up to £75 per brace in the bag.

which will be multiplied by the average annual number shot each season over the years. In the same way, a salmon fishery will cost up to £6000 per fish caught. A grouse moor is currently valued at up to £1200 per brace shot. To the sportsman who wishes to rent his stalking or shooting, these figures translate into anything from £200 to £700 per stag, and £40–£75 per brace of grouse.

Lowland

In lowland Britain, where the emphasis of land use is mainly farming, sport may be only one of several marginal activities which provide income, even if it is an increasingly important one. Game shooting is only one aspect of lowland shooting, but it is the most important in terms of estate finance. Pheasants, and to a lesser extent partridges and duck, form the bread and butter of game shooting and because most shoots rear and release their birds the quality of sport is what the owner makes of it. The value is expressed in the annual price per acre a landowner who owns the sporting rights might expect if he rented his land for shooting. Even if he had no birds on his land, or even suitable coverts, the potential alone may be as much as £2 per acre a year. On farmland where there is a good-quality established shoot that rental may rise to £5 or £6 per acre. On a 1000-acre farm this can mean an additional farm income of £5000 to £6000 a year. In terms of capital, it could add some £250,000 to the value of the farm.

An interesting example is provided by the 3000-acre Temple Estate near Marlborough, Wiltshire, where for the last three years a new shoot has been created by the Game Conservancy. The bleak Marlborough downland is not noted for its coverts. The Conservancy, the sport's research body, has planted 33 acres of sycamore, beech, pine and spruce, instant cover crops, and some four miles of

The damage (left), clearing up the mess (above) and replanting (right) after the great storm of 16 October 1987. Although it caused such devastation the storm did solve the problem of shoots where old coverts had ceased to serve their purpose of holding game.

hedges in strategic parts of the estate to hold pheasants and partridges. Initially the birds are being reared and released, but eventually the aim is to produce a wild-bird shoot. As a result the sporting rent has risen from £2 to £5 an acre over the 1500 acres so far developed, producing £7500 a year. Ian McCall, head of the Conservancy's advisory service and who has been in charge of the project, says that ten two-acre coverts planted to hold game on a 1000-acre farm without shooting can increase its rental value by £2–£4 an acre, each acre of woodland providing at least £100 a year regardless of the value of the timber.

The economic boom of the 1980s coincided with a decline in farm incomes and land values. This encouraged the creation and management of shoots, both to cater for increasing demand and to provide farmers with alternative sources of income. As the value of farmland declined, its amenity value increased. Estate agents selling farms, particularly in the south and midlands, found that potential purchasers were often far more interested in such factors as the quality of the house and its setting, the attractiveness of the landscape, and the possibilities for recreation, especially shooting. One agent reported that six estates had changed hands for the quality of the shooting alone.

If properly handled the government's Extensification Scheme to take 20% of UK farmland out of cereal production might have been more encouraging to shooting and wildlife in general. When the proposals were first published the Game

Conservancy argued that to take the land out of production as suggested would mean not only a 20% loss of habitat for wildlife in the cereal fields, but that the remaining 80% would be farmed more intensively to compensate for losing income from the other 20%. It would mean more sprays, heavier cropping, and fewer wild plants, butterflies and insects, small mammals, songbirds and game.

It also argued that under the Agriculture Act 1986 the government has an obligation to balance any legislation on farming with legislation to benefit conservation. It urged that the extensification proposals should be adapted to include conservation headlands, a system whereby strips around the edges of cereal fields are farmed using less harmful sprays and which has a proven record of benefitting wildlife.

So far the government has not accepted this. But it has provided generous grants, available from the Forestry Commission, Ministry of Agriculture, Farm Woodland Scheme, and district councils, to help with the costs of planting woodland. Ian McCall estimates that between 30 and 50% of the costs of planting at the Temple Estate have been met by grants.

The Costs

The value of shooting to the rural economy can be gauged only to a limited degree. It is not practicable to discover, for instance, the money generated by a wild migratory species like woodcock or snipe, because of their unpredictability. On most shoots they are simply a bonus, except in areas such as the west country where they appear regularly and it is worth organising shoots especially for them. For grouse, which because they are territorial and populations are easy to monitor and hence for driven shoots to be organised, the economics become more obvious. On pheasant and partridge shoots, where the success of the shoot depends entirely on the quality of the management, it is possible to get a far clearer picture of the economics.

For some years now the Game Conservancy has regularly analysed the costs of birds shot on up to 70 mainly lowground shoots. Pheasants make up 90% of the bag, with a few partridges and duck included, but the Conservancy concludes that it is impossible to separate the input costs between the three on most shoots.

The questionnaire sent to each shoot goes into considerable detail. As well as to the size of shoot, it establishes the area of wood, grass, arable and game crops, whether birds are wild, reared, or both, the numbers released and shot, rents and rates, the keepering costs analysed down to wages, housing, transport, clothing and equipment and the cost of dogs, equipment both for rearing and vermin control, the costs of egg, chick or poult production and release, of game crops, and the costs of beaters and pickers up including their wages, lunches and transport. In addition

John Hardbattle feeds Lord Clitheroe's pheasant poults. In 1988 each reared pheasant in the bag cost about £15.

shoots are divided into two categories, those which are owned and those which are rented, on the basis that those who have to pay rent for the land would have to face higher costs. However because some rented shoots are smaller, and the emphasis may be on do-it-yourself, it is possible to save costs so that the difference between the two categories is not often that great.

Their findings in 1988 were that the average gross cost of producing a shot bird was £14.91 on a rented shoot, and £14.05 on an owned shoot. The latter figure compares with £14.79 in 1986, £12.69 in 1984, and £10.04 in 1983. The costs are broken down into the rent and rates (£0.45 on an owner's shoot, £2.45 on a rented shoot), keepering (£6.89 and £3.68), equipment (£0.44 and £0.61), restocking (£3.12 and £3.81), post release feed (£1.53 and £2.65), game crops (£0.43 and £0.31) and beaters (£1.16 and £1.38) per bird.

Against this shoots can recoup some of their outlay by the sale of eggs, chicks and poults, and shot birds. This reduces the average net costs to £12.52 per shot bird on an owner's shoot, and £13.86 on a rented shoot.

The Game Conservancy does point out that although the proportions made up within the various sub-headings have not changed very much in relation to each other over the last five years, receipts from game shot were lower in 1988 than for the previous five years, indicating a flooded European market for shot pheasants.

The Game Conservancy has also produced premium costs, an average of the top 25% of the sample. In this the gross average costs per bird shot are £10.11 on an owner's shoot, and £8.89 on rented shoots, with net costs of £8.28 and £7.66 respectively.

LEFT *Research in action: Game Conservancy assistant Flora Booth takes a blood sample from a grouse shot on a Lancashire moor to check for louping ill.*

SHOOTING FOR SPORT

I N Britain the sport of shooting can be divided into seven sections, of which five involve live quarry. The other two are clay pigeon shooting, and target shooting. As well as driven game shooting there are rough shooting, wildfowling, pigeon shooting and stalking. Many who shoot live quarry with shotguns also shoot clay pigeons either for practice or in competition. The competitive branch of the sport, which has some 22,000 regular participants, has its own association, the CPSA, and rules.

Game Shooting

Game shooting involves the pursuit of any of the five species of gamebirds, pheasants, partridges, grouse, ptarmigan and blackgame, as defined by the Game Act 1831. Capercaillie, not officially defined as game but protected by the game laws, were once extinct in Britain but were re-introduced successfully from Scandinavian stock in the last century.

By one of those anomalies, snipe (officially a wader) and woodcock (a close relation which prefers forest habitats) require a Game Licence before they can be shot. The law governing hares (the Hares Act and Ground Game Acts) defines them as ground game, although there is no closed season and in most circumstances a Game Licence is not required. However the sale of hares is prohibited between 1 March and 31 July.

Game shooting can be carried out in two ways. Driven game shooting involves between six and ten Guns lining the edge of a covert (or in butts on moorland if shooting grouse, or screens or hurdles if shooting partridges) and having the birds driven over them by a team of beaters with dogs. Usually there are five to seven drives in a day. Driven game shooting involves a high degree of management and organisation.

The second method is by walking up through coverts or across moorland, with Guns interspersed between beaters, and shooting birds which are flushed. Although less formal than driven shooting, it also requires management to ensure that the birds are there in the first place. Although bags tend to be smaller, there is an added satisfaction of having had to work for it. As well as marksmanship, fitness and a knowledge of game and its ways also help. In Scotland the traditional way of shooting grouse, walking up moors over pointers and setters, remains popular.

LEFT *Partridges are shot from behind screens or hurdles or, as here, by Guns hidden from the view of approaching birds by a high hedge. This is the famous Sutton Manor shoot north of Winchester, Hampshire which was formerly owned by Lord Rank.*

RIGHT *On point: Champion setter Jack of Sharnberry remains motionless while William Town waits for the grouse to flush. Using pointers and setters is a traditional way of shooting grouse.*

Andrew Stock '89 ©

Rough Shooting

Rough shooting is the pursuit of game, wildfowl and other edible quarry not protected by the Wildlife and Countryside Act 1981, such as rabbits and pigeons, which may be present. Because the emphasis is on exercise and a bit of fun at low cost, it is usually an informal day out which takes place on rough land with a minimum of fuss and organisation. Expectations of the bag are low, marksmanship is at a premium, and any success is usually something to remember.

One problem caused by the current popularity of shooting is that many farmers with land over which rough shoots traditionally took place are trying to upgrade the shooting because of the increased income it could attract. Hopefully rough shooting will not decline because it has always been a traditional avenue of entry into driven game shooting.

Wildfowling

Wildfowling is the pursuit of wild duck and geese on the foreshore, as opposed to duck or geese flighting which takes place inland. Under the terms of the Wildlife and Countryside Act 1981 nine species of duck (mallard, teal, wigeon, pintail, shoveler, gadwall, tufted duck, pochard and goldeneye) and four of geese (greylag, pinkfooted, white-fronted [in England and Wales only] and Canada) may be shot. Of the waders golden plover and snipe may also be shot.

Because of its nature, and the element of danger, wildfowling appeals to a certain type of sportsman. The sport is at its best at dawn and dusk in deep winter, preferably when the weather is at its worst. To venture below the sea wall alone onto the wild and lonely saltings, to be able to recognise the possible flightlines of a wild and wary quarry, to remain motionless for hours on end with only the odd chance of a shot for the most part, and to make it back to the sea wall before a rising tide cuts you off, requires toughness, patience, a knowledge of wildlife and a love of lonely places.

Wildfowling takes place over large areas of land which have considerable conservation value, the majority of it designated as Sites of Special Scientific Interest or Special Protection Areas. For the most part the sport is extremely well regulated and organised through wildfowling clubs which are affiliated to the British Association for Shooting and Conservation.

Pigeon Shooting

Pigeon are vermin, the farmer's scourge, causing millions of pounds worth of damage to crops every year. Anyone who will help a farmer get rid of them is usually welcome. Traditionally pigeon shooting has been a poor relation, and sport could be had for a modest price or even free. Nevertheless because pigeon carcases are in demand, especially on the continent to where large numbers are exported every year, some farmers now charge a rent.

For those seeking pigeon shooting, success is not automatic. Farmers tend to be wary of those they don't know, and will want to ensure that anyone to whom permission has been granted to shoot pigeon is not going to take pheasants too. A well-planned approach is usually necessary.

Major Archie Coats, doyen of pigeon shooters: What it takes to decoy the wily pigeon successfully (above). A pigeon's view (below).

Stalking red deer: Colonel John Charteris at the end of a successful day on the Glenfeshie Estate.

Stalking

Although stalking is popularly associated with the red deer of the Scottish highlands, there are few lowland counties in Britain which do not have one or other species of red, roe, fallow, sika or muntjac. About 4000 people go stalking regularly. The sport appeals to many because it is a solitary sport which requires considerable fieldcraft. The key is being in the right place at the right time, and success is seldom a matter of luck. There are few better places to be than in a woodland clearing at dawn or dusk during summer watching the ways of wildlife, but the sport also continues through the winter months.

Because too many deer can damage crops, lowland stalking has increased steadily in popularity in recent years as landowners have benefitted from the rental, the sale of venison, and from the proper management of their deer herds. Also it was undervalued and ignored for many years, so visitors from the continent have been attracted by the quality of heads, particularly of roe.

WHO GOES

According to latest Home Office figures available (for the year to 31 December 1987) 861,300 people in Britain possess a shotgun certificate allowing them to own one or more shotguns. Four per cent of British men own a shotgun. Not all of them use their shotguns regularly, but according to the British Association for Shooting and Conservation some 600,000 do so, mostly after live quarry. Of these, three quarters go shooting on more than five occasions a year. Just under half the shotgun owners live in the country. More than a third are skilled manual workers, 22% are junior administrative and professional workers, 21% are semi-skilled workers, and 19% are employers, managers or professional people.

According to the same source, more than a half of those who use their guns shoot vermin. About 290,000 shoot pigeon, 160,000 shoot wildfowl, and 130,000 shoot game. Every year some 650,000 grouse, ten million pheasants, 600,000 patridges, 140,000 woodcock and 12 million woodpigeons are shot.

WHO PROVIDES

In *Shooting and Fishing in Land Use* Helen Piddington of the Department of Land Economy at Cambridge University undertook a survey of 45,000 landowners of 20 million acres, which represents about a third of the agricultural land and private woodland in Great Britain.

The results, published in 1980, showed that shooting took place on 58% of their properties, the frequency increasing markedly with the size of the holding. Shooting was most widespread in the east of the country and least frequent in the west, reflecting both the pattern of landowning and the favourable conditions and habitat.

WHERE

A breakdown of the BASC survey also reveals the major areas of shooting in Great Britain. For obvious reasons the wild species, grouse, wildfowl and woodcock, centre on the areas with the most favourable habitats. Hence grouse shooting predominates in Scotland, the north of England, Yorkshire, Derbyshire and Lancashire, with pockets in Wales. For some time now there have been insufficient numbers on Exmoor or Dartmoor for serious shooting purposes.

There are few counties in which woodcock are not found at one time or another. The most favoured areas are Cornwall and west Wales, where the habitat is ideal, and then Yorkshire, Lincolnshire, Norfolk and Kent reflecting the migrations from Scandinavia. Snipe also favour Cornwall, north-west Wales, Devon, Lancashire, Lincolnshire, Yorkshire and Northumberland.

Who provides: Hugh van Cutsem owns a famous shoot at Hilborough with mainly wild pheasants and partridges. Here he briefs his Guns, among them Charles Price II, the former United States Ambassador, Charles Price III, Major John de Burgh, Prince and Princess Albrecht zu Oettingen Spielberg.

For all species of duck the wetlands from south-west Scotland down to the river Mersey, and the east coast from the Humber down to Sussex, are the favoured areas. For geese the main area is between the firths of Moray and Forth on the east coast of Scotland, the Solway firth, Lancashire and Lincolnshire, and then Norfolk and Kent.

The grey partridge, which has declined sharply with new agricultural methods since the last war, is strongest in Cheshire, Lincolnshire, and then up to Durham. Kent, Wiltshire, Shropshire and Norfolk are also strong grey partridge counties. The red-legged partridge features strongly in Shropshire, the Midlands, from south Yorkshire to East Anglia, and Hampshire.

More woodpigeon are shot in Warwickshire and Essex than other counties, followed by Wiltshire, Gloucestershire, Oxfordshire, Kent, Norfolk, Cambridgeshire, Leicestershire, Cheshire and Shropshire.

The ubiquitous pheasant, second only in the national bag to woodpigeon, is shot in nearly all counties in Britain although Worcestershire and Shropshire predominate, with Hampshire, Wiltshire, Yorkshire, Lincolnshire and East Anglia not far behind.

Gamekeepers work long hours. Here Simon Remmington, head 'keeper for Peter Duckworth at Bleasdale, builds a sunken butt. Shooting provides full-time employment for some 12,000 people.

WHO SPENDS WHAT

Parts of the BASC findings were co-ordinated by the survey commissioned by the Standing Conference on Countryside Sports and undertaken by Cobham Resource Consultants. The Standing Conference, which meets twice a year, is attended by representatives of all field sports and the major conservation bodies, other countryside interests, and by ministries and government organisations concerned with the countryside. As well as being the think-tank of country sports, it is also able to communicate with the major areas of influence in the countryside. By providing badly-needed background information on field sports it has been able to counter ill-informed criticism of them and to help educate the general public about the role of the sports in the countryside.

The Cobham survey was produced in 1983, and if the financial values are somewhat dated, they do at least provide some idea of the scale of country sports and their contribution to the rural economy. In the years since then that scale has increased. According to Cobham, the total number of organisations which provided shooting – landowners, syndicates and clubs – was 52,000. Shooters spent annually some £212 million directly on their sport, from which 938 associated trade and service companies benefitted, and a further £175 million indirectly. Shooting provided direct employment for 14,500 people, and indirect employment for a further 9050. The sport generated £24.7 million annually in direct exports, and contributed £3.5 million a year to the government in the form of sporting rates.

If one considers that shooting is only one of the three major country sports, and second (after fishing) in terms of numbers participating, a clearer idea emerges of both sheer size of the country sports' contribution, and the difficulties they encounter in having to compete with other sports and pastimes which also share the countryside.

THE LAND GRAB

BRITAIN covers some 57 million acres. Over 40 million of them are farmed, although more than a third are unsuitable for cultivation and used mainly for rough grazing. Every year thousands of acres of countryside are lost to urbanisation – in the 1970s it was running at the rate of 62,000 acres a year although since then, with the amount of motorway building falling, the figure has dropped – and land is also lost to commercial forestry.

The dwindling remainder is faced with the challenge of accommodating not only country sports, but a host of other pastimes and activities. Recreation has been one of the boom industries of the last 20 years, and for the 83% of the population who live in towns the countryside seems an increasingly agreeable playground. As farming returns have decreased more farmers and landowners have sought to increase their incomes by offering leisure facilities. Shooting and fishing offer some return, but so do motorcycle scrambling, riding, caravan sites and theme parks.

A major problem facing landowners is how to channel visitors into the countryside so that they enjoy themselves, don't prevent others from doing the same, and don't spoil their surroundings in the process. Field sports are an ideal solution, providing control of access, income and education.

Fur, Feather and Fish

Cobham estimated that 3.7 million people go fishing and 214,000 go hunting regularly. Because the game fishing and game shooting seasons do not overlap and their venues do not clash, there is little friction between the two sports and many people participate in both.

However hunting shares both the season and land with shooting. In Britain and Ireland just under 450 packs of hounds hunt fox, hare, deer, mink, coypu, the drag

Some 3.7 million people go fishing regularly, although some are more successful than others and age is no guarantee of success.

and the clean boot at one time of the year or another. Although foxhunting proper starts on the first Saturday of November, hounds will have been cubhunting since the harvest is in and hare hunting will also be underway. So during the shooting season some 300 or so packs of hounds will be hunting two, three, and sometimes four days a week with anything up to a quarter of a million followers on horse, foot, car or bicycle. When hounds meet they attract more people now than at any other time in their history, a fact which causes some heartache to both sportsmen and farmers.

Fox and Pheasant

In the same way that the pheasant will not lie down with the fox, it can be said that shooting and hunting are not natural bedfellows. Foxhunting is older than driven game shooting; hare hunting and deer hunting older still; but the question of seniority cuts little ice in these hard commercial days. It costs a landowner money to mount a shoot, whereas horse and hound cross his land without charge, albeit with his permission.

However the key areas of potential conflict for sportsmen narrow down to two things. One is that foxes like to eat pheasants, and while many farmers are only too happy to have the odd fox around, no landowner with a shoot will tolerate too many. If the fox population is not controlled by the hunt then it will be controlled by the

The Hampshire Hunt hold their opening meet at Moundsmere Manor, where Mark Andreae has a top class shoot and foxes to hunt. Here the joint Master, Frank Momber, chats with head 'keeper Ben Knight.

Pheasants must share coverts with foxes, but birds disturbed by hounds will usually return. A week after this picture of a couple of Hampshire hounds flushing a brace of pheasants was taken at Moundsmere, 300 birds were shot from the same coverts.

gamekeeper, which sometimes means that the foxhunters have nothing to hunt at all.

The second point is that foxes share coverts with pheasants, and the last thing a gamekeeper wants is a pack of hounds crashing through disturbing his birds shortly before a shoot. In fact this complaint is sometimes overdone, especially if shooting is not imminent. Even if pheasants are disturbed and leave a covert it will not be long before they return, providing there is alternative cover for them close by. That there is little serious discord between the two sports nowadays reflects some hard work done at local level. For although there are areas of potential disagreement, there are far greater advantages in being allies.

One of the major changes in field sports over the last 15 years has been a more general realisation that unless country sports present a united front they will disappear. Many of the problems have been solved by a more tolerant approach among participants, and hard work by hunt officials to ensure that wherever hounds meet it will not clash with shooting dates and that hounds will not damage shooting interests. This message of mutual tolerance has also percolated through to most followers of country sports, and the result has been a more united front.

For shooting enthusiasts there are two general rules to follow. One is to protect the interests of other field sports as much as you would those of your own sport. The second is never, unless specifically requested to, shoot at a fox. Vulpicide is not the social crime it was in the last century (when the most appalling retribution fell on anyone in a hunting country who despatched a fox), but it is discourteous and may be very embarrassing for your host especially if, as always seems to happen on these occasions, your neighbouring Gun is a Master of Foxhounds. Furthermore if you shoot at a fox with a cartridge suitable only for a pheasant, your chances of killing it outright are slim. You will probably just wound it and it will eventually die painfully. Even if a host does ask his Guns to shoot fox, many turn a blind eye if Charlie comes through. It will probably be best if you do the same unless you are an excellent shot.

Puss

There was a time when hares were so numerous, and caused such damage to crops, that hare shoots were part of the rural calendar. While plentiful in some areas, modern farming practices have affected populations in others. Game Conservancy research indicates that shooting, hunting or coursing hares does not affect their populations. Although hares are accepted quarry on most shoots it is often wise to check with your host in case he allows either beagles or a coursing club over his land and so does not want them shot.

Reared birds now form the major part of the nation's annual game bag.

Reared birds now form the major part of the nation's annual game bag.

Changing Times

Compared with other countries Britain is rich in wildlife partly because climate and habitat are ideal; partly because of how our laws are framed; partly because circumstances and attitudes have developed a satisfactory and enduring form of management, evolved through a strong sporting tradition and sympathetic farming techniques which in the past sometimes came second to the game interests. Nowadays that sporting tradition is an increasingly important factor in the retention of habitat suitable for wildlife. That is because farming methods, in both the dairy and arable sectors, have become less compatible with the needs of wildlife since the last war. Despite the growth of the conservation movement, which in itself can cause problems by obscuring fundamental facts of life in the countryside, it is increasingly acknowledged that country sports help to retain a balance among so many conflicting and vested interests.

This message comes through clearly in Robin Page's excellent book *The Fox and the Orchid* (Boydell Press). The author, who is a farmer and journalist but who does not participate in any country sport, produces the most convincing evidence yet of field sports' role in protecting the countryside. Nevertheless to achieve this and to cater for the vastly increased numbers of people who have taken up shooting, game stocks do require comprehensive management. Without that there would be no shooting, game, or wildlife. One has only to travel through other countries where there is no such management to see that this policy works.

Most pheasants and partridges now shot are reared and released into the countryside before the start of each shooting season. Only on a minority of shoots do only wild birds exist. On most others the wild stocks are augmented with reared birds. Of the major quarry only grouse, woodcock, snipe and hare remain entirely wild.

Rearing and releasing birds was becoming common practice in the last century, and reared pheasants now form the major part of the nation's annual game bag. The operation is not particularly difficult, although techniques change. There are pitfalls for the unwary and it costs money. According to the Game Conservancy it now costs about £15 to produce each reared pheasant or partridge which is shot.

The advantage of reared birds is that you can make of a shoot what you want. With good advice, and the judicious planting of certain crops, shrubs and trees, you can create a shoot which will not only benefit the countryside and wildlife generally, but increase the value of your land.

The disadvantages are that it has changed the role of the gamekeeper. The preservation of reared birds has been substituted for the beneficial operations, such as vermin control, which went into providing the conditions in which wild birds other than game could also breed and rear young.

There are also worries that the releasing of birds may affect the breeding success of wild stocks. Current Game Conservancy research suggests that, although the number of reared pheasants has been increasing at an annual rate of 4.6% in the last 25 years, and the size of the bag by 2.3%, the contribution of the wild population to the bag has been decreasing. Their figures also show that if reared birds had the same rates of survival and breeding as truly wild birds, the national bag would be nearly double. But without reared birds the bag would be about one seventh of what it is now and pheasant shooting would not survive. Nor would the pheasant, and all the accompanying benefits to wildlife in general.

Nevertheless the wild pheasant or partridge remains the cream of the sport, and its value is reflected both in the quality of flying and in the price asked. Conversely, for all its advantages, the reared pheasant provides a major weakness in terms of good public relations.

Rearing and releasing pheasants and partridges should be undertaken in such a way and in such quantities as to give them time to adapt to their surroundings, be able to survive in the wild, and to learn the art of flight. It is a question of balance. Pheasants are adaptable; the countryside can absorb sufficient numbers to provide both incentive for shoots as well as the benefits for other wildlife. But there is a limit to the numbers that can be absorbed. Exceed it and you disrupt more than just the harmony of the natural life. It is a balance well understood by the keen shooting man, to whom an interest in the countryside and its wildlife is a main reason for going out with a gun. Without that balance the sport of shooting loses both its quality and its ethos. Instead it becomes a re-incarnation of the Edwardian shooting party but without the finesse, a packaged entertainment where the only object is to kill and success is judged only by the numbers killed.

There are similarities today with the latter part of Queen Victoria's reign. Game shooting has always attracted those who seek, or want to flaunt, social status. In modern Britain, with new-found wealth coming into the sport, it is not surprising that there should appear those who neither understand the balance, nor see the need for one, to enhance their status. Nor is it perhaps surprising that there are commercial shoots prepared to cater for them. After all, the costs of scale also apply to producing pheasants or partridges over Guns, and such days can be tailored according to market needs.

The result is the unedifying spectacle of a sea of pheasants (some of which may only have been put there on the day of the shoot) being driven through coverts to Guns driven from stand to stand, to large meal and back to stand, who know neither what to shoot nor how to shoot it, and are interested neither in the countryside they are visiting and what it contains nor the people who live and work there.

Questions must be asked about the ethics of two-gun days on shoots which only rear and release their game, and of rearing and releasing large numbers of non-game species such as duck for driven shooting. It is an image which shooting can and must do without. Little wonder there is talk of establishing a register of responsible commercial shoots.

KNOW YOUR QUARRY

I N Britain game shooting means the taking of certain live quarry with a shotgun, as opposed to stalking which means the pursuit of deer with a rifle. The term 'game' covers that group which, in law or tradition, are acceptable quarry. Under these two criteria it includes pheasants, partridges, grouse, ptarmigan, blackgame, capercaillie, woodcock, snipe and hare. All are edible.

There is also that all-embracing heading in the gamebook called 'various'. On a day's game shooting you may shoot woodpigeon, rabbits, jay, other corvids and vermin, although whether or not you actually do depends on circumstances. For instance on a driven day it is better to ignore rabbits, if only from the safety angle. Indeed you will normally be told 'no ground game' by your host. In any case, if your peg is placed back from the covert it is surprising how few you will see.

Not all game birds are indigenous. All except woodcock and snipe are members of the order *Galliformes*. Pheasants, partridges and quail (protected in Britain) are part of the same family (*Phasianidae*) and sub-family (*Phasianinae*). Grouse are a close relative. All three quarry birds also have two other things in common. They are sedentary as opposed to migratory species. They also prefer to run rather than fly, and will usually take to the wing only when there is no alternative.

The shooting seasons have been drawn up to end before the breeding cycle begins; with the pairing and mating in the early part of the year, and the hatching and rearing of broods through spring and into the abundance of summer sun and food. It starts again with the onset of autumn and continues through winter, culling the surplus which would not survive the cold and shortage of food.

Pheasant

All domestic fowl are descended from *Gallus gallus*, the red junglefowl, which is itself a pheasant and has a range from north-west India to south China, Java and the

Pacific islands which also reflects the range of the 48 pheasant species in the wild. There any similarity with the pheasant of the British countryside ends.

Although pheasants are alien to western Europe, they have adapted well and are found from southern Scandinavia throughout Europe except south and east Spain, Portugal, south Italy, and Greece. Precisely when they first came to Britain is uncertain. There is evidence that they were introduced by the Romans and they were certainly favoured by the Normans.

What is also certain is that the modern British pheasant is a mongrel. From the stock of Old English pheasant, descended from the Southern Caucasus pheasant (*Phasianus colchicus colchicus*) whose range abuts eastern Europe, it has been influenced mainly by the introduction of several species but predominantly three from the group known as True pheasants. These are:

a) the Chinese Ring-necked Pheasant (*P c torquatus*), which inhabits most of China and which is one of eight ring-necked species. Introduced to Britain from the second half of the eighteenth century its main feature, as its name implies, is its white collar;

b) the Southern Green Pheasant (*P versicolor versicolor*) is a strong flying pheasant first introduced from Japan in the first part of the last century;

c) *P c mongolicus*, sometimes also known as the 'Mongolian' pheasant although it does not in fact inhabit Mongolia, is one of the three Kirghiz pheasants found in the steppes from the Chinese border on the western edge of Mongolia to the Caspian Sea in Russia. That its territory knows extremes of weather has equipped this tough pheasant for adapting to British and European habitat. It was first introduced to Britain at the beginning of this century.

In addition to the 'British' pheasant there has also been a limited introduction of three of the ornamental pheasants:

d) Reeves's pheasant (*Syrmaticus reevesi*) comes from the forests of central China and was first introduced to Britain by John Reeves himself in 1831, although it did not become established until some time later;

e) Although Lady Amherst, wife of the Governor General and Viceroy of India, first sent her pheasant (*Chrysolophus amherstiae*) to Britain in the 1820s, it did not become established until the end of the nineteenth century. Its natural range extends from north Burma to the borders of China and Tibet;

f) The Golden pheasant (*Chrysolophus pictus*), from central China, has been in Britain since the first half of the eighteenth century.

Reeves's, a long-tailed pheasant, Lady Amherst's and the Golden which are ruffed pheasants, were introduced for aviculturists and to grace the parks and gardens of large houses. Some escaped to the wild. Stocks of purebred birds exist in Britain, but both Lady Amherst's and the Golden interbreed, and Reeves's and the

ABOVE *The pheasant is a bird of the woodland edge, and even reared birds have not forgotten.*

BELOW *Golden pheasant.*

56

The modern British pheasant is a mongrel.
Handsome, perhaps, but a mongrel nevertheless.

Golden have interbred with other feral pheasants occasionally, although the result is usually a 'mule'.

To return to the modern 'British' game pheasant the cock, reflecting the variations of colouring of its mixed ancestry, may be up to 35 in long of which about a half will be its tail. The drab hen, a shade of brown, is ten inches shorter. The pheasant is a bird of the woodland edge, seldom venturing further than 50 metres into cover unless there are sunny glades, and existing on insects, seeds, and fruits. According to Game Conservancy research the average British cock pheasant uses 500 metres of woodland edge for its territory and attracts up to five hens which may wander from one territory and cock to another.

Fighting between cocks for territory or hens can cause stress among the hens and affect their ability to breed (it also has a direct bearing on shooting policy; see chapter 13). In any case hens are not particularly aggressive or effective in the defence of their young and the large clutches, of up to 15 eggs, reflect the degree of predation.

The pheasant has become the workhorse of modern game shooting, superceding the grey partridge, partly because it has adapted better to modern farming conditions and is ideal for driving from coverts, and because it is easier than the grey partridge to breed and rear for stocking purposes. According to the Game Farmers' Association, which represents most of the major game farmers in Britain, some 15 million pheasants are released onto shoots every year. They join a wild stock estimated to be a million.

Grey partridges used to be the main quarry bird of sportsmen until replaced by reared pheasants. Because of farming pressures they are now in decline.

Grey Partridge

Partridges are a valuable addition to a shoot. They provide testing shooting, and a contrast to the ubiquitous pheasant. And because the partridges' closed season ends on 31 August, they extend the lowland shooting season by a month in law and virtually two months in practice.

Three species of partridge can be seen in the British countryside. The indigenous grey partridge (*Perdix perdix*), favoured by British sportsmen from the seventeenth century, is found throughout Europe except parts of Norway and all but the north of Spain, and eastwards to Asia. Until the development of pheasant rearing in the last century, it was the main quarry bird of British sportsmen.

In Britain its range is extensive except in the north and west of Scotland, and parts of Wales and Ireland. A bird of downland and farmland it has been in decline in this country since the last war. The reasons are complex, but basically involve the interaction of changing methods in farming, removal of the hedgerows along which they nest, the use of chemicals and fertilisers which affect the supply of food and cover, and increased disturbance. The bird has become something of a symbol, an indicator of the impact of farming methods on the countryside, and as such the subject of intensive and long-term research.

As a result the Game Conservancy (the grey partridge is its logo) started a cereals and gamebirds research project on farmland near Basingstoke in Hampshire in 1984. It has shown that if farmers do not spray their cereal headlands, the improved habitat for the grey partridge, not to mention other game birds, songbirds, small mammals, butterflies and a host of other insects and plants, is very significant. The Game Conservancy has been urging the government to use these findings in establishing its set-aside policy for cereal farmers.

The grey partridge is not widely reared for shooting – the adaptable red-leg is far more suitable – and its numbers continue to decline overall with the population now around a million birds. Most shoot owners tend not to shoot grey partridges unless the local population can stand it.

In flight the grey partridge is distinguished by its rusty-coloured head, grey breast, and horseshoe mark on its underside. It eats seeds, leaves and insects, and sawfly larvae are particularly important for chicks. It is said that the shooting fraternity will know in Royal Ascot week in June what sort of wild partridge season it will be. If it is wet and cold, affecting the insect supply, the chances of survival among the young decrease.

In contrast to the pheasant the grey partridge cock is monogamous, a loyal and attentive partner, and a protective father which helps with the rearing process. For her part the hen is an assiduous mother, and will defend her brood stoutly.

Partridges provide testing shooting and extend the shooting season. Here Senator William Flowers, from Georgia, tackles Sutton Scotney's best.

Red-legged Partridge

As its name suggests the slightly larger red-legged partridge (*Alectoris rufa*) has red legs, a rufous tail, and a black necklace extending from eye to eye around the throat. Its traditional territory covers south and west France (hence its other name, French partridge), Spain and north-west Italy.

Although Charles II is credited with first introducing the red-leg to England, it was not until a century later that it was introduced in sufficient numbers to become established. Preferring the drier sandy and chalk soils it has established itself mainly in the east and south of England, the midlands, with pockets in Wales, the north of England and Scotland.

To the sportsman red-legs present two advantages. Although they share the habit of using legs more with the pheasant than the grey which flies more readily, when they do take to the air they fly strongly. The second is that they are fairly easy and cheap to rear and release compared with grey partridges.

In the wild the red-leg shares many of the grey's qualities as mate and parent. But it does differ in that the hen may lay two clutches of up to 15 eggs in separate nests, one for the male to incubate. This, too, is nature's way of compensating for high mortality at the chick stage.

The red-legged partridge is an immigrant. Its other name, the French partridge, is a reminder that its natural home is south and west France, Spain and north-west Italy.

The Chukar hybrid

According to the Game Farmers' Association some 10–15 million partridges are reared and released every year, and a current problem is their precise identity. A fair proportion are not in fact purebred, but a cross between red-leg and the chukar partridge (*Alectoris chukar*), a native of the Middle East and Asia.

The cross-breeding first took place in the 'sixties in Sussex following experiments in Italy. Not only is it even easier to rear and breed than the red-leg, but because the cost of producing a hybrid is about half that of a pure red-leg, the majority of partridges released on shoots are crosses to some degree or other.

The Wildlife and Countryside Act 1981, introduced to conform with European legislation, states that no hybrid may be released into the wild. Game farmers were granted an extension until October 1987 (subsequently extended until 1989) because there were insufficient stocks of purebred red-leg birds.

After release the hybrids breed in the wild, but the game farmers say that they do no harm to the environment. The Nature Conservancy Council asked the Game Conservancy to undertake research into whether or not they compete for food or territory with either wild red-leg (which the Department of the Environment seems to think are indigenous) or grey partridges.

Research undertaken during 1988 tends to show that the hybrids do not breed as well as the pure-bred red-legs in the wild, and are detrimental to wild red-leg stocks on shoots. The NCC has recommended to the DoE that the licence to release chukars and hybrids should be phased out over the 1989–90 and 91 seasons, and a decision is awaited. However if, as a result, the DoE insists on banning the hybrid, it will certainly affect partridge stocks for the next few years until numbers of red-legs build up.

If they do it will also provide another headache for shoot managers and game farmers, for if interpretation of the Wildlife and Countryside Act leads to a ban on the release of hybrid partridges, what about pheasants? They are surely the most hybrid game bird of all.

Grouse

The red grouse (*Lagopus lagopus scoticus*) is said to be Britain's only truly unique species. To many it is the most challenging of the game birds, its fast flight hugging the contours a match for any Gun and the wild and attractive surroundings in which it lives adding to its allure. One thing is certain: it is the most expensive of the game birds to shoot.

During the excellent 1988 season, on some moors which were achieving bags of

500 brace a day, a party of eight Guns would have received a bill of more than £40,000 by the time VAT was included. The bill facing each Gun for the day would thus have exceeded £5000. But that price is no deterrent. Most sporting agents agree that it is as difficult to find good grouse shooting for their clients as it is to buy a good grouse moor.

The red grouse inhabits the uplands of Britain up to 2500 ft, north of a line from Bristol to Humberside, on Dartmoor and on Exmoor. Long regarded as a species particular only to Britain, it is in fact a subspecies of the Willow grouse (*Lagopus lagopus*) of northern Europe and north America.

Red grouse live in heather, the young ling heather providing adults with the bulk of their food along with bilberry and crowberry. They also need grit and water, and the chicks need insects initially. Grouse are mainly monogamous, the cocks staying with the hens through the rearing process, and the family stays together as a covey late into the year.

The main attraction about grouse shooting is that the sportsman is pitting his skill against wild, wary, fast-flying quarry. There is nothing artifical about grouse except the degree of management which surrounds them. They do not lend themselves to rearing in captivity, and so wild populations cannot be augmented.

Consequently moor owners go to great lengths to ensure the proper management of their stocks. Ornithologists and conservationists are unanimous that the species would not survive without the management provided by shooting, and without it the heather moorland, and everything that lives in it, would disappear under forestry or sheep. The government also takes that point of view.

Grouse are a prime example of how the fortunes of a bird have flourished with the development of shooting. The clearance of Scotland's traditional forests, followed by the intrusion of the railways, the increasing popularity and enjoyment of its fabulous sporting potential and the development of the breechloading gun, gave the grouse a status before which both sheep and crofters were forced to give way.

But the management of a wild bird such as the grouse has never been easy. It has required intensive research, and enormous input in terms of both money and labour. At the turn of the century such was the significance of grouse, and concern at decline of stocks, that a parliamentary committee of enquiry was set up that led eventually to Lord Lovat's thorough report entitled *The Grouse in Health and in Disease*.

The concern is still with us, for grouse continue to face formidable pressures. There are the traditional ones of predation from foxes, weasels, crows, eagles, hen harriers and peregrines, and the need for a constant supply of food, water within reach, and grit. Nowadays there are the additional problems of grazing by sheep and cattle which affects their habitat adversely, and disturbance from walkers.

Grouse are prone to the diseases of strongylosis, carried by the parasitic trichostrongyl worm which lowers resistance to infection from other diseases and affects chick survival, and to coccidiosis. Overcrowding, with its effects of encouraging disease and on food and territory availability, produces population crashes.

So the key to management is to ensure that there is an optimum breeding population for the ground available; optimum conditions in terms of heather for food (young) and cover (older and longer) and the insects essential for chicks in the early weeks, grit and water; ruthless predator control within the law; and that the surplus grouse are shot to leave the optimum breeding population. No wonder the management is a tricky business and that the costs are substantial. It is not surprising that with ever-increasing costs of labour since the war the standard of moor management has generally declined and the grouse stocks with it, heralding the spread of forestry. Commercial forestry, with its tax incentives, makes continual incursions into the four million acres of moors in England, Scotland and Wales which hold grouse.

The problem is particularly severe in Scotland and emphasises the economic significance of grouse to estate incomes. According to the Game Conservancy a Scottish estate with a successful flock of sheep must shoot at least 65 grouse per 1000

Grouse: 'Its fast flight hugging the contours is a match for any gun . . .'

acres to remain solvent. On an estate without sheep this figure rises to 142 per 1000 acres. Within the last decade English moors have been above these thresholds; Scottish estates have at best been close to them or below.

But decline or not, the grouse remains the supreme sporting bird. In addition there are grounds for optimism, one of which stems from that very decline. Because of the degree of management over the years, moorland has become a haven for other species beside grouse, and is now regarded as an internationally important habitat. This endows the moors with a mantle of interest from national and international conservation and government bodies outside the field of shooting.

Furthermore the 1987 season was excellent in England – probably the best since the last war, and the best in Scotland for nine years. The recovery of grouse stocks in Scotland in 1987 was continued into 1988 with the result that the shooting season there, and on English moors as well for that matter, was also one of the best for a long time. As well as giving heart to moor owners it has also added impetus to research programmes. Valuable research into whether or not the grouse's territorial behaviour affects populations has for some time been undertaken by the Institute of Terrestrial Ecology at Banchory.

Grouse research also received a valuable boost when the Game Conservancy undertook its North of England Grouse Research Project from 1979–86, and started a similar project in Scotland in 1985. The results of both are now beginning to become evident. For instance while it has long been held that grouse populations are subject to predictable cycles, there was increasing concern that Scottish stocks did not increase from 1980 despite some good breeding years. Research indicated that the reasons for continuing low population levels might not be cyclical but due to high winter losses. It has suggested to moor owners that particular attention should be paid to predator control.

The Project has also carried out research into dosing birds against the trichostrongyl worm which affects both chick survival and winter losses of birds. From this a medicated grit, coated with a substance containing an anti-worm drug available only on veterinary prescription, has been developed. Under strictly controlled conditions it has been placed on moors where the results are being monitored. Initial results at Nidderdale and Wensleydale in the north of England, in Dumfriesshire in south west Scotland and in Inverness-shire, have been promising. In some cases the parasite burdens have been halved and, most important, the breeding results have been very encouraging. The next stage is for the grit to become available commercially.

TOP *Hen ptarmigan in autumn plumage.*
MIDDLE *Cock in summer.*
BOTTOM *Hen in winter.*

Ptarmigan

You have to work hard if you want to shoot ptarmigan, for *Lagopus mutus* is a cousin of the grouse which usually lives up around 4000 ft. Be prepared for a good climb to get to the top, and traversing the scree when you get there can be hard work. But the scenery can be spectacular, and even if not successful you can console yourself that the view was worth the climb anyway.

The birds survive on heather, crowberry and bilberry. Their colouring, greyish brown in summer but pure white in winter except for black on the side of the face of the cock and on the tails of both sexes, provides effective camouflage which is needed given the lack of cover.

Ptarmigan are monogamous, the male helping with the rearing and aggressive in defence of the family although some may desert after hatching. Hens usually lay up to about ten eggs in a breeding season which is limited by the foreshortened summer, the young either dispersing or staying with the hen until late autumn.

Shooting is by walking up. Probably because they are unused to humans, ptarmigan have a tendency to stand and stare at you indignantly before they depart. Like grouse they would prefer to leg it but when they do take off, which is inevitable because of lack of cover, they fly strongly and hug the contours which make them a testing shot. Care must be taken when shooting to ensure that sheep are not present and also that, when hit, the bird can actually be retrieved – which is often easier said than done.

Although once found in Wales, Cumberland and south-west Scotland, ptarmigan are now restricted to north Scotland. However because of their comparatively inaccessible habitat numbers do not appear to be declining. Ptarmigan are also found in Norway, the Pyrenees and Alps, Iceland, Greenland, and northern America.

Blackgame

Once found in many parts of the British Isles until the turn of the century, the blackgame's habitat is now confined mainly to Scotland, north west England and Wales, with pockets in the south west and Staffordshire. The species (*Lyrurus tetrix*), which is also known as black grouse, is also found throughout Scandinavia, eastern Europe and Asia.

One of the reasons for blackgame's previously wide range is that it can cope with a variety of habitats including woodland fringes, plantations, rough and marshy land, and upland. As these habitats have disappeared, so have the blackgame. Nevertheless they have adapted to changing conditions in their existing habitats, but while it is true that in their good areas there is reasonable stability their status does give cause for concern. Basically they have declined dramatically through their range and are only faring reasonably at the extremities of it. New plantations may also have been a help to them.

Blackgame can cope with a variety of habitat including woodland fringes, plantations, upland and rough and marshy land – whether Guns can cope as well is sometimes questioned.

Blackgame eat a variety of foods, from the buds of Scots pine and heather to potatoes and insects. The blackcock is distinguised both by its black feathers and lyre-shaped tail (which may account for the fact that it does not particularly like flying downwind). The greyhen, although similar to a red grouse, is larger, has less rufous plumage, and has a forked tail. Secretive and wily, they are strong and fast fliers when they do get up despite their cumbersome appearance.

Blackgame are noted for their elaborate courtship displays. The lek is the site at which cocks congregate and undertake their famous challenging display from March, hens joining them in April to mate, after which cocks appear to play no part in the rearing process.

A three-year research project into the habitat requirements of black grouse to provide practical advice for timber growers and moor owners has been started by the Game Conservancy's Upland Research Unit at Crubenmore.

Capercaillie

If blackgame appear cumbersome, capercaillie (*Tetrao urogallus*) are more so, a cock bird measuring some 34 in compared to the blackcock's 21 in, and the hen is correspondingly larger than a greyhen. The largest of our feathered quarry, it is not in fact defined as a game bird in law, although it is regarded as such, because it did not exist in Britain when the Game Act 1831 was passed.

Although indigenous, it is thought to have become extinct in England in the latter part of the seventeenth century, and in Scotland and Ireland a century later. Re-introduction took place in the nineteenth century, Lord Breadalbane introducing more than 50 birds from Sweden to Aberfeldy. Because the main habitat is pine forest, populations suffered with the need for timber during both world wars.

Shooting is usually by driving, and sometimes on driven pheasant shoots in Scotland a capercaillie will loom over the Guns like an out-of-place turkey. It would be as well to check with your host beforehand whether or not he wants them preserved, and don't forget that their season closes a day earlier than pheasant shooting. Despite their bulk, capercaillie tend to be secretive birds, but when airborne they are fast fliers. The cocks are particularly sought by continental trophy hunters.

Woodcock

Of all lowland quarry the woodcock is the most exciting and one of the most difficult to shoot. It is the subject of more dining clubs in Europe and America than any other bird. In Britain there is a dining club run by *Shooting Times*, the sporting magazine,

Andrew Sloth '89

for those who achieve a right and a left at woodcock. It is no mean achievement; the woodcock's sudden appearance and elusive, weaving flight make it particularly difficult to hit in singles, let alone in twos.

Nevertheless the woodcock (*Scolopax rusticola*) is an anomaly. It is not legally a gamebird, but you need a game licence to shoot one. It is classified as a wader, but its legs are short for one, and anyway it lives in woodland. It is also a bird woven into lore, casting its spell in Europe, north Africa, Asia, and America as well as in this country.

Whether or not it actually does carry its young between its legs in flight is still a topic which fills the letters pages of the sporting press, but there are many eye-witness accounts. Our forbears thought that woodcock spent their summers on the moon, possibly because there are lunar influences on migrating patterns, and woodcock have an uncanny ability to foretell and keep ahead of bad weather. Quite why our predecessors regarded the woodcock as slow-witted is anybody's guess, although it may have been because the bird was relatively easy to trap in those days when hunting for the pot was more important than any sporting ethic.

Most woodcock appear during pheasant shoots, when the cry " 'cock forward" can be guaranteed to put Guns on their mettle. Out of covert and in open countryside – if it flies that way, for often it will slip down rides, back over the beaters or jink round the sides of a wood and away before walking or flanking Guns can react – the woodcock is not a particularly difficult shot. It appears slow and somewhat ponderous compared to, say, a partridge when flying in a straight line. But in woodland the woodcock is at home. Its colouring provides perfect camouflage on the leafy woodland floors it prefers. It requires dry ground for nesting, evergreen undergrowth for shelter, and wet areas for feeding where it can sink its bill to probe for the worms, beetles and other insects that make up its diet.

The population in Britain is made up both of residents and migrants. Woodcock appear in most parts of the country but the largest bags occur in Norfolk, which provides both good habitat and first landfall for birds migrating from Scandinavia and north-east Europe, the western part of the country and Ireland where migrating birds find the habitat ideal.

Woodcock usually provide nothing more than a pleasant bonus during a day's shooting, but from time to time their numbers provide another element of their unpredictability. On occasions they may be present in force due to migration or weather – when the woodcock are 'in' in Cornwall news spreads among the sporting fraternity like wildfire. Although there is concern when bigger bags than usual are shot, research indicates that this does not harm woodcock numbers. Large numbers of woodcock die every year from natural causes. There is a shootable surplus, and no indication that shooting pressures affect the breeding population adversely. Woodcock populations generally are not under pressure. Even in hard weather, when the shooting of wildfowl, waders and woodcock is banned, there are strong arguments that to continue shooting would not affect overall woodcock populations providing the birds are not affected directly by the cold. The main arguments to stop shooting woodcock are when, as a result of a long journey or extreme cold, they are suffering the effects of starvation and exhaustion. In which case large numbers will probably die anyway.

According to the Game Conservancy's National Game Census for the 1987–8 season, woodcock bags were still much higher than in the 1960s, but 20% less than in the peak year of 1984. In the west country numbers were high.

Snipe

Snipe have two distinctions. They are very difficult to shoot and, because two of the three species are protected, you will need to be able to identify them correctly. The law permits you to shoot only the common snipe (*Gallinago gallinago*).

Snipe belong to the *Scolopacidae* family, which includes curlews, godwits and sandpipers and which are distinguishable by longish bills to probe for food, long legs and angular wings. Woodcock also belong to this family, but to a different sub-family on their own.

In fact you will rarely come across the two protected species, great snipe

Andrew Stock 89 ©

(*Gallinago media*) or the jack snipe (*Lymnocryptes minima*) during a day's shooting. The great snipe is larger and darker than the common snipe and has some similarity to the woodcock. It has more white on the edges of its tail than the common snipe. Mainly a summer visitor, it shares with the other two a marshy habitat when it breeds, but is otherwise found on drier land such as fields and heaths. The jack snipe is the smallest and has a shorter bill. Alone of the three it has no white in its tail feathers. It breeds mainly in Scandinavia and is a migrant.

The common snipe is a partial migrant, visiting birds to Britain coming from northern Europe. However the species is found throughout the world and breeds in most temperate and sub-arctic zones in the northern hemisphere. There are also species of snipe in the southern hemisphere. They are widespread in Britain, particularly in those areas which have not suffered from agricultural drainage. Because of their food requirements snipe are usually found where the ground is soft, in bogs, marshes, watermeadows and sewage farms. Often they are in small groups, or wisps. Snipe breed throughout the summer. They usually lay four eggs and after hatching may divide the brood to lower the chances of an entire brood being lost.

Because their eyes are set back in the head snipe see danger coming and flush quickly – sometimes out of shot. When put up they fly close to the ground in a zig-zag, which makes them so difficult to shoot, and then they rise quickly. One of the dangers of snipe shooting is that you need quick reactions to get a shot in, while at the same time making sure that it will be a safe one. This is probably the inhibiting factor, as well as the erratic flight, which makes snipe so difficult to hit. Locals in the

Snipe usually lay up to four eggs and, after hatching, may split the brood between male and female to lower the chances of an entire brood being lost.

west country, which is noted for its woodcock and snipe shooting, will tell you that for every snipe accounted for seven cartridges may be fired.

On driven snipe shoots experienced Guns often turn their backs to the direction from which the birds are being driven, allow them to cross the line of Guns, and shoot them going away. They argue that it is safer because they will have checked their field of fire and because the birds have had time to gain height, and the angle between Gun and bird decreases.

Hare

Although still healthy in many places, brown hare numbers have declined overall since the 1960s because of farming changes. The National Game Census shows a decline in the bag of from 12 per km^2 to about 2 per km^2 in the last 30 years. However their numbers are still sufficient to need controlling and, unless your host wants you to refrain (he may also want to cater for the hare hounds or the coursers), it is usual to shoot them. But it would be as well to check at the start of the day.

Hares and rabbits belong to the order *Lagomorpha* and family *Leporidae*. The brown hare (*Lepus capensis*) exists throughout the world. It inhabits most of Britain (it is not indigenous to Ireland but was introduced there) up to 1600 ft above sea level. It is found on open farmland and sometimes woodland, is mainly solitary except in the breeding season, and lives entirely above ground.

Attitudes to hares vary between those farmers who regard them as a nuisance, and the hunting and shooting fraternities who do not want to see their numbers drop. In many counties a cloak of mystique, not to say witchraft, used to surround the hare, for it is a great survivor. Long ears give it excellent hearing, it has a keen sense of smell, and the eyes set back in the head provide a wide area of vision. If threatened it may well clap – keep a remarkably low profile – until you practically step on it.

It can run fast and has considerable stamina. Its agility, coupled with virtually all-round vision, make it very elusive. People who go coursing will vouch for the fact that even at full speed hares change direction at right angles when pressed by the greyhounds. There is one famous occasion (captured on film) during a course at Altcar when, in full course, the hare did a backward somersault over the pursuing greyhounds to evade them and make good her escape.

In Britain the mountain, or blue, hare (*Lepus timidus*) which is also found in Greenland and North America, is confined mainly to the highlands of Scotland and to Ireland. Although it has also been introduced to the Western Isles, Wales, the Pennines and Yorkshire, it thrives in the heather uplands of Scotland because what is good for the grouse is also good for the blue hare.

It is mainly distinguised from the brown hare by the blue-grey summer coat and white coat in winter. It also has shorter ears and it does not have the brown hare's black tip to the tail. The Irish subspecies has more russet in its summer coat, and does not turn white in winter. Blue hares have a reputation for being bolder than brown hares.

Unlike all the other quarry you are likely to encounter on a day's shooting, both species of hare can be shot all the year round except, like game, on Sundays and Christmas Day. If you are an owner or occupier of the land, or are duly authorised, you do not require a Game Licence to shoot them. Hares may also be shot at night. Neverthless you cannot sell hares, dead or alive, between March and July inclusive.

Although still healthy in many places and in need of control, brown hare numbers have declined overall since the 1960s because of farming changes.

THE SEASONS

The seasons for shooting most wild quarry are clearly defined in law, and failure to observe them is an offence. The closed seasons have been established to allow each species to breed and rear in peace. They take into account the habits of each bird as well as the climate and habitat in which they live.

The shooting seasons, coinciding with the time of year of bad weather and shortage of food, are designed to allow the shooting of the surplus which would in any case perish, leaving sufficient to breed the following season.

The shooting season starts on *August 12*, with grouse, ptarmigan and common snipe. Blackgame come into season on *August 20*. On *September 1* the partridge season opens, and woodcock can be shot in Scotland. It is also the start of the wildfowling season, during which pinkfooted, greylag, Canada and whitefront (the last named in England and Wales only) geese, and gadwall, goldeneye, mallard, pintail, common pochard, teal, tufted, shoveler and wigeon can be shot. The seasons for golden plover, coot and moorhen also open. *October 1* sees the start of the pheasant season, although it will probably not get underway in most places for a few weeks until the leaf is off the tree and undergrowth has died back. Woodcock shooting also starts in England and Wales.

Grouse, ptarmigan and blackgame seasons close on *December 10*. Capercaillie, woodcock, common snipe, coot, moorhen, wader and duck and goose shooting inland and above the high water mark close on *January 31*. Pheasant and partridge shooting continue only for another day, until *February 1*. On *February 20* wildfowling below the high water mark of ordinary spring tides finishes.

It is illegal to shoot any of the game species out of season, on Sundays, Christmas Day, or between the hours of sunset and sunrise. In Northern Ireland the grouse season extends only until 30 November, the season for hares is from 12 August to 31 January, and partridges, hen pheasants, and barnacle, brent and Canada geese are protected at all times. In England, Scotland and Wales there is no close season for hares, although they may not be sold from 1 March to 31 July. Rabbits and hares may be shot at night by authorised persons.

There are some species which have no close seasons. They include rabbits, woodpigeons and feral pigeons (but not racing pigeons!), collared doves, great and lesser blackbacked and herring gulls, carrion and hooded crows, jackdaws, rooks, jays and magpies, starlings and sparrows. It is also necessary to control stoats, weasels, mink, brown rats, foxes, feral cats and grey squirrels.

Most other avian and ground species are protected by law, and it is an offence under the Wildlife and Countryside Act to kill them.

GUNS, CARTRIDGES AND ACCESSORIES

F OR game shooting you will need a double-barrel shotgun, ie one which will fire two cartridges without your having to reload. From there on the matter becomes more complicated because there is a wide choice of sizes, makes, and prices. The Firearms Act 1968 dictates that for you to own one on a Shotgun Certificate, the barrels must have a smooth bore and be longer than 24 inches. Most standard shotguns have barrels of beyween 25 and 30 inches. Under Section 2 of the Firearms (Amendment) Act 1988 some pump or self-loading shotguns may require a Firearm Certificate.

But to continue with the basics. It would be better to stick to a hammerless ejector, a gun on which the hammers (or tumblers to give them their correct name) are inside rather than outside the action of the gun, and which ejects the cartridges automatically when you open it to reload after firing. Above all you must make sure that the gun fits you. Gunmakers will measure you for a new gun, and when selling you either a second-hand gun or a mass-produced gun a reputable dealer will ensure that it does fit.

You can choose either a single-trigger model, on which you do not have to move your finger to a second trigger to fire the second barrel, or a double trigger model. On two trigger guns the front trigger is for the right barrel, and the rear for the left. Two trigger models are best for game and rough shooting because they provide a choice of choke. Some people argue that because the single trigger mechanism is more complicated there is more to go wrong with it, a charge hotly denied by those who use them. The right barrel will fire first, although on many modern guns it is possible to select which barrel should do so.

Unless you plan to attend a large number of double-gun days – when you expect to use two guns on each drive – it would probably be better to restrict yourself to a single gun at least initially. Nevertheless if you can afford a matched pair you will always have a spare handy in the event of the gun you are using breaking down in the field.

New or Used

In making your choice you face three decisions. The first will be whether or not to buy a gun which has been mass-produced or hand made. A mass-produced gun will be comparatively inexpensive, tough and workmanlike and, if it is machined to high accuracy, should be reliable. Some can be hand-finished to a higher standard. There are no makers of mass-produced shotguns in Britain, and most of those that are imported come from America, Spain, Italy, Belgium and Russia. For under £1000 you could expect to buy a new imported shotgun. You would certainly have a wide choice of second-hand guns.

Above all the gun must fit you, and a try-gun will be used to measure you.

Best Guns

Best English guns are hand-made and are among the finest examples of craftsmanship in the world. A new one is expensive – you must expect to have pay more than £20,000 – but once you have used one you will never want to shoot with anything else. It also holds its value. At Sotheby's Gleneagles auction of guns last year a matched pair of Purdeys finished just after the last war fetched £35,200. A pair of Holland and Holland 'Royal de Luxe' 12-bores made for the 1983 Game Fair fetched £38,500. In all the 173 lots achieved £685,000, which averaged out at just under £4000 per lot.

A gun with a full cross-over stock, enabling its user to shoot from the right shoulder but left eye.

From the moment you order your gun from a top English gunmaker you must expect to have to wait for two to three years for delivery. There are no shortcuts. Once you have decided the gauge of gun, whether it is to be a side-by-side or over-and-under, and any special requirements or engraving, you will first be measured with the help of a try-gun. This is a special adjustable stock which can be adapted to measure both your shape and size, and also to take account of which eye you use to shoot with.

Most people have a master eye, which may or may not coincide with the master arm. If you shoot from the right shoulder and your master eye is your right one, the stock will not require much, if any, deviation off a straight line. However in certain circumstances the stock may need a cast; it will have to have a curve made in it so that when you mount your gun the barrels will align with your master eye.

Once the measurements have been taken, the work will probably take no fewer than 750 hours. Your gun will represent the combined skills of a number of qualified craftsmen – barrel filer, actioner, lock maker, ejector maker, engraver, stocker,

RIGHT *A craftsman at Purdey's works on a straight hand stock.*

BELOW *A beautiful pistol grip stock at Purdey's awaits final assembly. The encrusted bottle contains the firm's magic formula for finishing and polishing.*

furniture maker and finisher. Each will have served at least a five year apprenticeship and some longer. Some firms have their own apprenticeship schemes. Each craftsman qualifies only in his own skill. There are no formal qualifications, but the kudos of having completed an apprenticeship with a leading gunmaker is sufficient qualification in itself.

Given unlimited time anyone could make something which would operate as a gun, but the skill of the manual craftsman lies in his ability to shape steel to tolerances of a thousandth of an inch, quickly and without mistake. Even so, it may take a barrel filer up to 50 hours to reduce the two nickel steel machined forgings to a pair of finished barrels.

The basic design of the sidelock action has not changed much in 100 years, and the actioner will impress his own influence on his work because he will have made all the tools he uses himself. The engraver can easily take 70 to 80 hours to engrave a standard fine rose and scroll on a best sidelock. Other more ornate work, such as large scroll and carved work, would have an undetermined time spent on them and would merely be a question of cost.

Most stocks for English game guns are straight in style for single trigger guns, as opposed to pistol grip, and the fore-end either splinter or beavertail, the wood coming from the root of best old walnut trees which have long outlived their use as providers of nuts and oil. Birds eye maple was used at some time in the past, but it is walnut which is not only best for the job but which has such superb figure. The

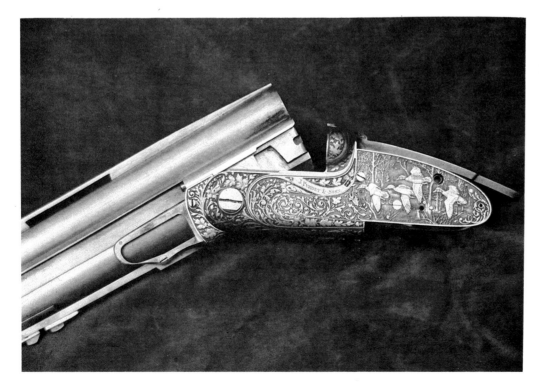

An engraver can take 70 to 80 hours to engrave a standard fine rose and scroll on a best sidelock. But special engraving by a master like Ken Hunt, as on this Purdey over and under, will take longer and cost more.

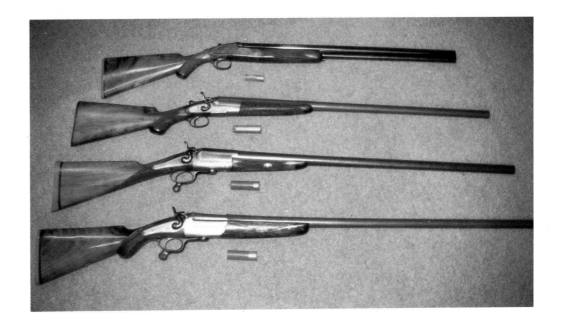

Four specials, from the top: A single-trigger 20 bore over and under by Purdey (price, second hand, £28,000); a 10 bore Willis trap gun designed for live pigeon shooting; a Hooton Jones 10 bore; and a massive single barrel 8 bore by Holland & Holland.

traditional centre for buying the walnut blanks is the Dordogne in France, but the wood nowadays comes from much further afield all around the Mediterranean and even from America. Once it has been completed the finishing alone, with a mixture of beeswax, linseed oil and paint drier, will take about four weeks.

Your gun will pass from one craftsman to the next and back again until barrels fit action and action fits stock, for the furniture maker to provide the triggers and such additional items as the lever, and for the finisher to ensure that the timing and the regulation of the mechanism are right.

The gun may have gone through two stages of proofing, one for the individual 'Provisional' tube before assembly, and a final 'Definitive' proof for gun and action together. The action will have been case hardened, and the barrels and furniture blued. What you receive is not only a gun which works perfectly and which gives you the aesthetic pleasure of a piece of supreme craftsmanship. There will be no other gun like it, for each component will have the individuality of the skilled craftsman who made it, and will integrate only with the adjacent component it was made for.

Second Hand

Although there are now only a very limited number of shotgun and rifle makers in Britain, many fewer than there used to be, the gun trade has a strong tradition and is regarded worldwide as the centre for 'best' guns. As a result you need not buy a new gun; there are a great many second-hand British guns of excellent make on the market for under £5000, together with skilled craftsmen available to adapt and service them. Make sure, though, that you do not buy a gun which is too old. However well it was made, metal and wood wear out in time.

Over-and-Under or Side-by-Side

The second choice you will have to make is between a gun with over-and-under or side-by-side barrels. As the name suggests, the first has barrels mounted one on top of the other and, although they are made by one or two of the best gun makers (they are more expensive) from time to time, they have never become popular for driven game shooting in England.

Possibly because of its aethestic look, lightness, for reasons of tradition, or simply because it is easier to reload, the side-by-side shotgun has become synonymous with driven game shooting in Britain, with English made sidelocks or boxlocks highly favoured. After all, the sporting gun trade and driven game shooting developed at the same time, and the side-by-side had a good start before the over-and-under first appeared at the turn of the century in modern shotgun form although, perhaps surprisingly, the over-and-under system predates the side-by-side.

Bores, big and small

The third choice you will have to make is the size of gun. This is expressed as a bore or gauge, and the method of measuring it goes back to the earlier days of gunnery when the projectile was measured in pounds. The best description of how it works

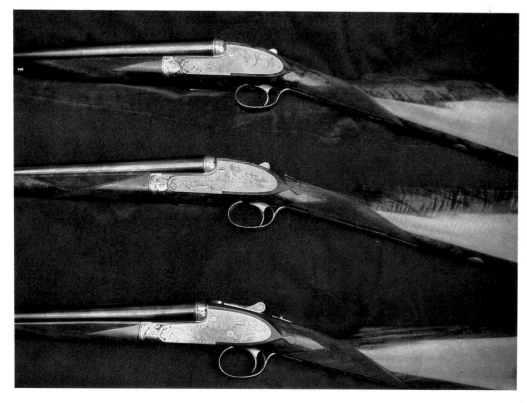

An unusual matched set of three single-trigger side-by-side sidelocks by Purdey's – 12, 20 and 28 bore – with game scene engraving.

comes from Major Sir Gerald Burrard's classic book *The Modern Shotgun*: 'The size or gauge of a gun depends on the diameter of the bore, but this is not measured in decimals of an inch as is done in the case of rifles, but is denoted by the number of spherical balls of pure lead, each exactly fitting the bore, which go to the pound'. An eight-bore would take eight, a 28-bore 28.

The heavier bores, such as four, eight and ten, are frequently used by wildfowlers. The size most commonly used for game shooting is the 12-bore, although 16-, 20- and 28-, because they may be lighter yet still effective at most ranges, all have their devotees. If you are a good enough shot, you will kill cleanly with any of them. A standard 12-bore side-by-side chambered to take a 2½-inch cartridge with a 1¹⁄₁₆ oz load, will weigh about 6½ lb. A 12-bore magnum may weigh up to 8½ lb. A 20-bore, depending on the load, may weight from 5½ lb upwards.

Most older English shotguns have chambers to accept cartridges of 2½ inch. Most modern ones take 2¾ inch. You can use a 2½ inch cartridge in a gun chambered to take a 2¾ inch cartridge, but never try the other way round. Using a 2 inch 12-bore cartridge, although safe, is not recommended in longer chambered guns. Magnums, any shotgun which has a chamber or special proof rating designed to accept a larger than standard load, are especially useful for wildfowling. But for most driven game shooting a standard cartridge with a standard load will suffice. Indeed it may give better results.

A selection of .410s. Great for boys and, unfortunately, for poachers as well.

Actions

You will also have to chose whether or not you want a boxlock or a sidelock action. You will notice the difference on the lock plates: those of a modern sidelock extend under the bar of the action and backwards roughly the length of the top lever into the head of the stock. The rearward end of most boxlock actions finishes in a straight or scrolled edge against the stock. Most boxlock actions, based on the Anson and Deeley design, are simple and reliable and because they are cheaper, make for a less expensive, workmanlike gun. It is, however, less elegant than the sidelock.

Best guns are nowadays mostly sidelocks. Most of the orders received by the top gunmakers are for side-by-sides, and the majority are for 12 bores.

Parts of the Gun

Although you may not want to concern yourself with how your gun works, you will need to know the various parts of it so that you can can take it apart for cleaning and putting away in its case, not to mention being able to hold your own about guns in conversation.

A side-by-side is made up of three main elements, the stock to which is attached the action, the barrels and the fore-end. The stock, the part you put to your shoulder, is made of wood, usually walnut. The top is the heel and the bottom the toe. The top edge is known as the comb, which leads to the grip, which is usually chequered to prevent your hand slipping.

There are four basic types of stock of which two, the straight hand and the half pistol grip, are more commonly used for game shooting. The full pistol grip and the Monte Carlo are more commonly seen in clay pigeon shooting.

On the top of the grip immediately behind the top lever will be the safety catch, and then the lever itself for opening the gun. Underneath are the trigger guard and triggers. On the sides are the lockplates. The vertical face where the ends of the barrels meet the stock is the action through which the two strikers appear. The area in front of them and almost at right angles is the action flats and bridge which joins them together.

On the front extremity or knuckle are the two cocking levers, or lifters, which cock the gun automatically when the gun is opened, and the extractor cam which activates the primary extraction for each barrel. On an ejector gun the spent cartridge cases will be thrown out automatically. On a non-ejector the extractor will withdraw the cartridges slightly so that they can be taken out.

Fore-ends vary between the splintered, which is lighter and elegant and is used

These three stocks are, from the top, a straight hand on a Dickson Round Action, a pistol grip on a Purdey sidelock, and a half pistol grip on an Anson & Deeley boxlock.

Smoking, to ensure action fits barrels.

on many British guns, and the beaver-tail used on some overseas guns which is more substantial and provides better protection against hot or cold barrels.

It will have recesses to accept the cocking levers or lifters of the action and normally houses the ejector mechanism and bolt loop of the barrels. It is held on by a spring-loaded bolt and, with the common Anson style of fore-end bolting, the gun is dismantled by pressing the button at the end of the bolt to remove the fore-end so that the barrels and the stock and action can be separated.

On the underneath of the barrels are the two lumps including the hook, flats which usually carry the proof marks, and loop. On the vertical face are the breech, and the cartridge extractors.

Choke

The choke, at the muzzle end of the barrels, is a restriction indiscernible to the naked eye, built into the barrel which affects the concentration of shot as it leaves the barrel. It thus determines how wide the pattern spreads through its range, and for how far it is effective.

Choke is measured by the percentage concentration of the shot pattern in a 30-inch diameter circle at 40 yards. A barrel with no choke is known as true cylinder. Improved cylinder will place 50% of the pellets within that circle, quarter choke 55%, half choke 60%, three quarter choke 65%, choke 70% and full choke 75%.

Choke is a matter of personal choice and experience, but on most game guns the right barrel is either true or improved cylinder, and the left about half choke. On many modern over-and-under guns and some side-by-sides it is possible to adapt the choke by screwing a different one into the end. The same degree of choke has the same effect with all bores. But remember that just because a barrel measures a degree of choke it will not necessarily shoot that pattern. It is a matter of trial and error to discover which cartridge performs best in any given gun.

Cartridges

Basically modern cartridges contain in precise measures all those ingredients – lead shot, wadding, powder to propel the shot, and the primer to ignite the powder – which in times gone by had to be prepared and loaded separately.

The materials used nowadays in the casing are non-corrosive and watertight, so that cartridges will remain usable for a long time providing that they are stored in an even temperature. One change in recent years has been the plastic cartridge case which means that they are unaffected by damp. However, the plastic cases take a very long time to disintegrate if left on the ground, so it is as well to pick up your spent cartridge cases and take them home with you rather than leaving them out in the countryside. Another recent change has been to replace the old overshot card with a crimp closure on the ends of the cartridge, which is claimed to lead to more consistent patterns. The new wadding is plastic rather than cardboard.

The cartridge industry is intensely competitive, and you can often get a good discount. You may expect to pay anything from £2 upwards for a box of 25 12-bore game cartridges. In addition to making sure that the price is right, you will want to reassure yourself on two other points. One is that the make is reliable. In fact there are very few cartridge makers, and many retailers simply overprint one or other of their products with their own name. The second is that you have chosen a cartridge with the correct shot size and characteristics for your purposes.

Cartridges and their loads are a science on their own, and there are many people who prefer to load their own to obtain the combination of shot size and charge which suits them best, especially if they are not available commercially.

The shot size is usually printed on the cartridge case. The number of pellets inside a cartridge depends on the weight of the charge of shot and the size of shot used. The *Eley Shooters Diary* gives useful tables showing the number of pellets in any given loading. They range in 17 sizes from a single spherical ball up to dust shot, but the ones most used for birds range from BB and 1–7. In fact from BB up to 3 are used mainly for geese. On hare you would expect to use 4–5, for mallard 4–6, for most game birds and woodcock 6 or 7, and for snipe 8.

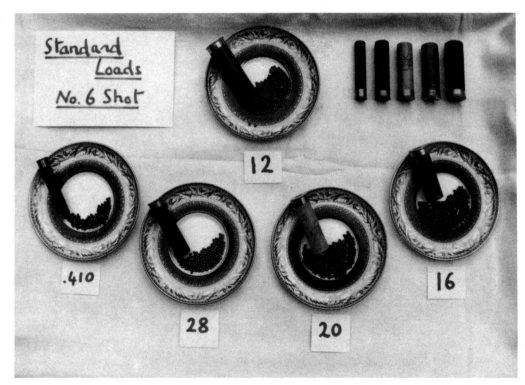

Standard loads using number six shot. It illustrates why a young shot has far more chance of success with a 28 bore than with a .410, and why father has even less excuse to miss with a 12 bore.

The most popular all-round size is 6. The standard English game load is 1⅛ oz of shot, which means that each cartridge contains 287 pellets. Number 5 would contain 234 pellets, and number 7, 361 pellets. From October 1989, under the Rules of Proof 1989, all measurements became metric except in certain very limited instances.

When taking up shooting it is probably best to choose a gun which takes standard cartridges. As you become more experienced you may want to experiment and see if other guns or loads are more suitable for you. However good shooting is very much a matter of confidence. If you are shooting well, don't change, because the moment you begin to harbour any sneaking doubts about your gun or your cartridges, however unfounded, they will affect your performance.

NECESSARY ACCESSORIES

You will also need a gun case and slip, cartridge bag, cleaning kit and gun cabinet. A solid case in which to carry your gun will reduce the risk of damage and make it less conspicuous in public places.

Under the Firearms Act 1968 it is an offence to have a loaded gun in a public place. Even if not loaded, guns in public make a sensitive issue and the police don't like them. Nor do they like your gun left in full view in your car. Much better to have it locked away in an inconspicuous case.

Most gun cases, in leather, metal, or composite materials, are designed to carry a gun broken down to its three main components with a separate compartment for each. There is also usually room for gun cleaning kit. For between £50 and £200 you should have a wide choice.

The slip protects your gun between drives during a day's shooting. Getting in or out of vehicles or crossing fences it is surprising how the opportunities for damage arise, and the slightest knock may do damage. Slips range from simple canvas to leather with wool or some other lining. Handles can be useful, but ensure that there is a shoulder strap. Prices range from £20 to £120.

Cartridge magazines to take large quantities of cartridges are still available, but are seldom used nowadays because it is easier to put a case of 250 in the back of a car and transfer them from there to cartridge bag. Cartridge bags, made of stout leather or canvas with a fold-over flap which buckles down and with a shoulder strap (there is quite a fashion for them among the girls as handbags), are available in sizes to take 50, 75 or 100 cartridges. It does save carrying them around in your pockets, although on reaching their pegs many Guns transfer cartridges from bag to pocket for speed of reloading. Depending on material or size, a bag will cost between £20 and £120.

A leather or canvas cartridge belt, which will take 25 cartridges and cost approximately £15 to £30, can be useful if the sport is fast and furious and you have to fall back on reserves. However it comes into its own more when either walking up or rough shooting, when the last thing you want to be encumbered with is a cartridge bag or bulging pockets.

Cleaning a gun at the end of each day's use is essential if it is to remain reliable, safe and to retain its value. The cleaning kit you will require is a cleaning rod to which can be screwed a bronze brush, a jag for holding cloth patches, a lambswool mop, and a silicon cloth, gun oil and a stock finish. You can either buy them separately to keep in your gun case, or alternatively as a complete kit in their own box, and you should be able to obtain everything you need for under £100. It is also useful to have toothbrush and pipecleaners to remove dirt from nooks and crannies and chequering.

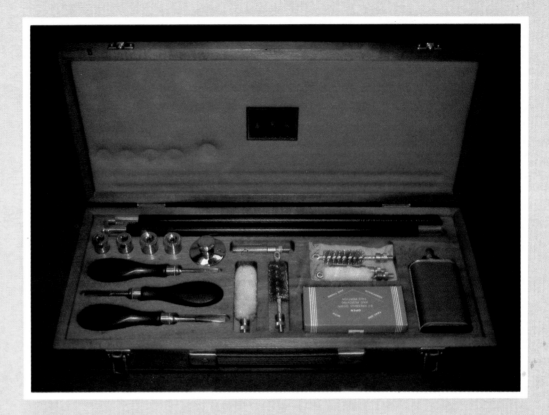

You would also be wise to buy three accessories which you will need sooner or later. You should never fire your gun without cartridges as it may cause damage to the strikers. Snapcaps (approx £10) are dummy metal cartridges which allow you to squeeze the trigger without fear of damage to the action. Even if your gun ejects cartridges automatically there is always a chance, however small, that one may become stuck and it is useful to have a cartridge extractor (under £10). On days when you expect to do a lot of shooting, either with one gun or two, the barrels will become hot and you will need a handguard (under £20), a leather-covered guard which slips over the barrels and allows your front hand to hold them.

What used to to be common sense is now law. The new Firearms Amendment Act, which became law in 1988, now requires you to lock your gun in a safe place. On how satisfactorily you do this may depend the number of shotguns the police allow you to hold. What is or is not a safe place is open to interpretation, and even some gun cabinets may not pass muster in certain police forces. The best course of action is to ask the firearms officer of your local police force the specifications they require (preferably in writing), and to go then to a reputable local gun dealer. Unless you have an arsenal it need not be expensive to buy a suitable cabinet and have it installed, and you should find what you need for less than £200.

SHOTGUN CERTIFICATE

Before you own a shotgun you must have a Shotgun Certificate from your local police force. Some self-loading and pump action shotguns require a Firearm Certificate, as do rifles and revolvers. No gun dealer will let you depart with your gun until you have the requisite certificate.

A shotgun certificate is obtained by applying to the police, and costs £12. It lasts for three years, and costs £8 to renew (both prices may rise shortly). Some police forces remind you that it needs renewing, but not all do and the onus is on you to remember.

Until the law was amended recently the police had to supply you with a shotgun certificate unless they could show that you were unfit, either because of your mental state or because you had a conviction. Over the years, though, it has become obvious that the police are keen to control the numbers of shotguns in circulation, and some have tried to impose their own restrictions on the granting of shotgun certificates.

The Firearms (Amendment) Act 1988, introduced in the wake of the Hungerford shootings, made important changes which are now being implemented. Most significant, police need not now issue or renew a shotgun certificate unless they think that you have a good reason to possess a shotgun. However the onus is on the police to show that you do not have that good reason. To want one for sporting and competitive shooting, and vermin control, is sufficient, and indeed the police cannot refuse you even if you do not intend to use the gun. Whoever verifies an application for your certificate has to state that they know no good reason why you should not have a gun. The Act also provides that applications for both shotgun and firearm certificates must be accompanied by four photographs of the applicant.

The Act makes four other important changes. You are now under statutory obligation to keep your shotguns in a secure place – common sense, perhaps, but you would be surpised how many people do not. The second is that although there is no statutory limit to the number of shotguns you may own, each shotgun will need to be identified and listed on your shotgun certificate. Third, you will now have to produce your shotgun certificate when you buy ammunition. Fourth, self-loading and pump-action shotguns will require a firearm certificate unless they are adapted to hold no more than two cartridges in the magazine and one in the breech.

GAME LICENCE

Before going to shoot game, woodcock and snipe you will also need a Game Licence, obtainable from most post offices for £6. The fact that many Guns

Loading instruction on a Game Conservancy course for young shots. Few, however, will have the opportunity to use a pair of guns again during their shooting careers.

forget to buy one is no excuse, and they are breaking the law. You do not need one shooting wildfowl or vermin, or hares providing that you are the owner or occupier of the land or the one person allowed to be authorised by them.

INSURANCE

You will also need to arrange third party insurance. Membership of the British Association for Shooting and Conservation automatically covers you for £1 million.

OVER AGE

Although there is no lower age limit for obtaining a shotgun certificate in England, Scotland and Wales, there is for the possession of a shotgun and ammunition. Providing he or she has a valid shotgun certificate, anyone over the age of 17 may buy a shotgun and ammunition. From the age of 15, providing you have a valid shotgun certificate, you can be given or lent a shotgun and ammunition, and use them without supervision but you may not buy them. Anyone under the age of 15 may not be given a shotgun or ammunition but, providing they have a valid shotgun certificate, can use them under the supervision of someone over the age of 21.

Simon Clowes dressed for the covert side: Smart, practical, warm and comfortable.

8

WHAT TO WEAR

To some on the shooting field dress is critical. They judge and will be judged on appearances. Nevertheless we probably worry far too much about what other Guns think of our clothes and it is probably a sign of experience when we do stop worrying. At the same time there is nothing worse that feeling out of place and it is true that appearing neat, tidy and correctly dressed adds to confidence. In addition you owe it to your host.

There are also important reasons for the correct choice of clothes, because they may affect your shooting ability. You must be warm and dry. You will not be able to shoot straight if you are so frozen or wet through that cold and misery have numbed your brain and you are late onto birds, your feet won't move, or your fingers fumble with the safety catch.

At the same time you will not want to be too hot. It is extremely unpleasant toiling through heather bowed down by coats and jerseys on a balmy summer day. The problem with driven shooting is that it involves little movement. Although you may seem warm enough by the time you arrive at your peg, it is suprising how the cold can get at you if you stand still or sit for a few minutes. One tip is to make sure that you have the right clothes next to your skin and always to wear them; you can add or shed outer layers as conditions dictate.

Although the strict conventions of dress are more relaxed these days, they do still exist for the aspiring Gun. The main reason for this is that those who shoot regularly find out through experience that the 'uniform' does its job. You will be hard put to find alternative clothes which do it any better. Guns will recognise if you have not learned this lesson, and judge your experience accordingly.

The 'uniform' is not based on whim nor only on the experiences of the comparatively few generations which have enjoyed driven game shooting. Fashions may change, but the materials and sombre colours are based on centuries of hunting in all its forms and survival out of doors. But however dull the greens, browns and greys which match the colours of the countryside, it is surprising the touches that can make your appearance more jolly and individual without seeming gaudy or out of place.

There are two other points to bear in mind. Don't buy clothes which are too tight. You don't want them too loose either, but it is undignified to have to struggle in mud or be unable to climb over a gate because your breeks cling to you, or to be unable to swing with your birds properly because your coat is too tight.

Second, natural fibres such as wool, cotton and silk generally do the job far better than most man-made fibres, although advances in materials such as Goretex and Neoprene (used for mountaineering and wetsuits respectively) are being used increasingly successfully.

From top to toe you will have to consider:

The Hat

Headgear may come in or out of fashion in other walks of life, but in shooting the hat is essential. More body heat is lost through the head than any other part of the body (which is why, in the days before house heating, our ancestors wore nightcaps). Second, a hat will shield your eyes from rain or glare. Third, it will help shield your upturned face from approaching quarry. Gamebirds are neither blind nor deaf. The next time you see a pigeon flying towards you look up and it will probably veer away.

Although there is a handsome variety of floppy brimmed sporting hats, the experts say that the English gentleman still prefers the 'flat hat' – the conventional tweed cap – for shooting. The trilby seems to be making a comeback; days were when the Gun wore the trilby and the gamekeeper the cap. Among the younger generation of Guns there is the odd bush hat or two, but by and large the majority of Guns you meet on a day's driven shooting will be wearing caps. Although they also come in loden, waxed cotton and corduroy, tweed remains the most popular.

Skin Deep

Don't forget that you may be standing or sitting in the open for long periods. On a driven day opportunities for moving about are limited. On a cold day consider cotton, silk or thermal underwear, including longjohns or combinations. If you get too warm during the day you can always shed outer clothing.

What you wear around your throat will keep you warm and dry. Conventional Guns stick rigidly to the custom of collar and tie. A cotton or wool-cotton mix shirt is best, and check patterns are popular. Some Guns prefer a cotton polo-neck shirt. The important thing is to have something fairly tight around your throat, without it

Experts say that the English, and in this case Scottish, gentleman still prefers the conventional tweed cap, Christmas decorations and all.

Waiting for the partridges this American visitor sports, not altogether seriously, the all-purpose 'hunting cap' complete with radio and ear plug.

Out shooting you will see a variety of eye-catching headwear and stockings, although seldom both on the same person.

being restricting, to keep both wet and cold out. It is also worth wearing a scarf or investing in a towelling cravat to keep the rain out; some Guns carry a spare in their pocket to change.

The next layer may be either a sleeveless V-neck pullover or jersey, or a heavy sweater. There is currently a great fashion for sweaters among those Guns who have opted not to wear jackets. They come in a variety of patterns and colours and cut something of a dash. Some Guns prefer a thermal waistcoat instead or as well because of the extra pockets.

Suit Yourself

For formal driven days the shooting suit, with jacket, waistcoat and breeks, retains its pre-eminence. Nevertheless a visit to the tailor these days is not taken lightly, and even an off-the-peg suit can cost about £200. Many Guns make do with a combination of breeks, jersey and shooting coat, and they are perfectly acceptable.

Although you won't want your breeches to be too tight, they should not be too baggy either. Plus-fours went out of fashion on the shooting field because in the rain they became a sponge which flapped uncomfortably around the knees. For up to £50 you should be able to equip yourself with breeches. Although available in corduroy, moleskin and loden, tweed still seems to have the edge for driven days.

For formal driven days the shooting suit retains its pre-eminence. Mr and Mrs Robert Bell wear the traditional greens and browns with style.

95

If you buy a jacket to shoot in (as opposed to an ordinary sports jacket which you can slip on if you go into the house for lunch), either separately or as part of a suit, make sure of three things. One is that it allows you room to move – some shooting designs have shoulder gussets to allow for this. Second, make sure that the side pockets are reinforced so that you can put cartridges in them if necesssary. Third, that the buttons are sewn on extra strongly.

At Ground Level

Socks can also add a bit of colour. You will see reds and blues and yellows among the greens, browns and beiges, and stripes and checks and plenty of bright patterns (although those in the know seem to think that the fashion has moved on from stripes). You can also buy brightly-coloured garters – selling like hot cakes last season – and let the ends hang discretely below the tops when rolled down.

Whether you fasten your breeks over your socks, or under them, is a matter of personal preference although if you have colourful sock tops it seems a pity to hide them away. On the other hand, girls sometimes prefer to button over so that they can roll their sock-tops over their knees for extra warmth. Always buy wool socks. They are by far the warmest, and warmth stays in the body if your feet are warm. Once you begin to feel the cold creeping into your feet and up your legs you won't get warm again until you go indoors, so what you wear on your feet is very important.

Snappy stockings: Christopher Hindley, Nicola and Simon Clowes and loader John Weir at Lord Clitheroe's Downham estate.

There is no need to be cold. Leather is warmer than rubber, and many Guns swear by stout leather shoes or boots which come over the ankle. Soles are either studded, or with thick rubber treads. An extra pair of undersocks can be worn. Alternatively you can fall back on the ubiquitous rubber boot (green is still tops, although brown, blue and deep red appear from time to time) in which case be sure that you equip yourself with padded undersocks.

There are also lined rubber boots and the ones which seem to be the most effective of all combine the warmth of a leather lining and the practicality of a rubber outside. Although a pair of leather-lined rubber boots may cost more than £100, they will keep you warm and dry and they are fitted with zips to help you put them on and take them off.

Perfect for keeping you warm and dry. Leather-lined rubber boots, worn here by Diana Dent.

At Your Fingertips

It is also vital to keep your hands warm. Although your coat will have many pockets, you can guarantee that the moment you put your hands in them a bird will come over. There is also the element of safety if you have your loaded gun in the crook of your arm and both hands in your pockets. The best answer is gloves or mittens. Guns tend to have very definite ideas about what to wear on their hands. Whatever you wear must allow you full control of the gun, and your trigger finger must be free.

Many Guns use leather gloves, lined with silk, with a hole through which they can put their trigger finger when the drive begins. Wool gloves with leather palms are also popular. Other Guns swear by mittens, either leather or woollen. Millermits, the green and brown woollen mittens with string palms to help grip, remain very popular and comparatively inexpensive.

It is also possible to get handwarmers, either in the form of a metal box in which a stick of charcoal burns, or small packs of chemicals which when shaken produce constant heat for several hours.

The Outer Layer

The right choice of shooting coat is important because it is expensive and with proper care should last for many seasons. You get what you pay for but there is a wide choice and you need to be clear in your mind just what you want.

In their choice of coats Guns tend to fall into one of four categories. Those with shooting suits often carry a lightweight waterproof. The second group swears by waxed cotton coats, which for more than a decade now have ruled the roost of fashion in the country (and also in the middle of London). A third group goes for a tweed coat with a padded lining. The growing demand for Loden coats, with their soft wool which resists rain, indicates a dent in the British resistance to European fashions. Some are available with thermal and waterproof interlinings. The fourth group experiments with man-made fibres such as Goretex which keep you dry and warm but, because they 'breathe', prevent you from boiling.

You may have to pay £100 to £200 for your coat, although you may get what you want for less. It is not an item to economise on. Whatever your choice, it is worth considering a coat with a detachable lining so that it will be just as useful for keeping you dry while walking up grouse in the summer as keeping you warm while standing by a covert-side in deep mid-winter.

The other thing to remember is that as long as it suits you, don't worry about what other people might think.

Ear Protection

While you are equipping yourself, you must give some thought to protecting your hearing. Some Guns don't wear any form of protection, either because they haven't had reason to think about it (yet), because some ear protectors tend to impair their shooting one way or another, or simply because they forget.

If you don't wear any form of ear protection you will go deaf, and the more you enjoy your shooting the quicker it will happen. When it happens, there will be absolutely nothing that anyone can do about it. The chances are that if you are exposed to constant noise of more than 90 decibels (a decibel is a unit used to compare intensities of sound), it will affect your hearing. If you stand near a jet at full power, you expose yourself to 130 decibels. Shoot with a 12-bore shotgun and you could expose yourself to the same or more every time you squeeze the trigger. Because of the complex way in which the decibel system is graded, this could represent a noise anything up to 1000% greater than 90 decibels.

Normally your ears, if they are healthy, allow you to hear a wide range of sounds very accurately. They are complex and very highly sensitive in order to interpret the wide range of vibrations they receive. The sound of a gun will destroy the thousands of nerve endings which receive these vibrations and transmit them to the brain as sound. You will begin to find that you cannot hear conversations easily if there is background noise. The first to be affected are the high frequencies, which usually means that you will not be able to detect the consonants easily and hence be unable to hear a conversation completely or accurately. It is the consonants which convey the meanings of words even if it is the lower-frequency vowels which give them their weight. In consequence you will find that you become self-conscious about taking part in conversations – either in business or socially – for fear of making a fool of yourself and begin to withdraw into yourself. It is a very gradual process but even

A water-proof kilt has many advantages over leggings or overtrousers. This one is worn by Captain Kenneth Woods.

if you give up shooting it accelerates as you get older. You will find that the first to be affected is the ear opposite the shoulder you shoot off.

You may also find that you suffer from Tinnitus, a singing in your ears which, apart from being unpleasant in itself, signifies that your hearing is impaired. If, at the end of a day's shooting (or your children complain after a noisy disco) there is singing in the ears, you will know that the noise level you have been exposed to has inflicted damage. Even if the Tinnitus goes away the next morning, it is too late.

So there is a very real risk of deafness from shooting. The problem is that it is a gradual process and you may not notice it until your other half or your children comment on it. By that time it will be too late. Although a hearing aid may help you (and even that may simply amplify the jumble of noises) your hearing won't return to what it was. All you can do is to take immediate steps to halt the decline, and urge others to ensure that they take precautions.

Any shooting instructor worth his salt will tell you the same thing, although they tend to disagree over what the best form of protection is. The important thing is to prevent the vibrations caused by loud sounds from entering the ear canal and getting to the 30,000 or so nerve ends. If you totally block your ears it is surprising how much noise will penetrate through the skull. That does not matter; it is the vibrations which do the damage.

There are two types of protection, ear muffs and ear plugs. Both have their adherents.

Ear Muffs

Ear muffs, which link over the head and make you look like a disc jockey, cover the whole ear thus preventing the vibrations from entering. They range in price from about £10 to more than £100 for a pair which will allow selected noises through. The most modern incorporate microphone and amplifier, together with a shut-off device which operates automatically when a gun is fired.

The advantages of muffs are that they are bulkier than ear plugs so that you shouldn't lose them, and if they work they work very well indeed. They may also help to keep your ears warm. The early prejudice (for no good reason) against wearing them for game shooting has disappeared, so you can wear yours without feeling self-conscious. If anyone does pull your leg about them, the chances are that more Guns will agree with you than with him.

They do have disadvantages. They are more expensive than plugs. They must fit absolutely tightly to be effective and may not do their job properly if hat, long hair, beard, spectacles or whatever are in the way. Their bulk may also either affect or inhibit your shooting when you bring the gun up to your shoulder, but if everything fits properly this should not happen.

Coats made of Goretex fibre, and electronic ear protectors, are among recent developments in shooting wear.

Ear Plugs

Plugs can be just as effective as good muffs if they fit properly. However the ear's canal can vary from person to person, and rigid plugs may not work with some people. There are plugs made from plastic foam which adapt to your ear (issued to servicemen by the Ministry of Defence) which are regarded by some people as very effective. Others can be specially made to fit the exact shape of your ear.

Among the advantages of plugs are that they are cheaper than muffs. You can buy most for less than £10. Some people also find that they affect their shooting less – it may be that they do not block out all sounds so that hearing can still play its part in alerting the Gun to a flushing bird. However plugs are small, and can be lost easily. In addition they may compress wax in the canal, and are not advisable for anyone who has an infection of the ears.

Possibly the best solution is to wear both plugs and muffs. But if you do nothing about it, or put cotton wool in your ears in the belief that it will afford you protection which it won't, you will go deaf and consequently miss much in life. And under no circumstances whatsoever should you allow children to accompany you shooting without providing them with adequate ear protection.

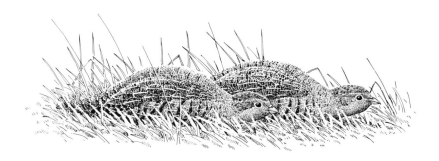

LEARNING THE ROPES

BEFORE you go shooting you will need to know what happens off the shooting field as well as on it. On the shooting field it really boils down to understanding the sequence of events and learning how you fit into them, how you are regarded by other people, and marksmanship. However it is also necessary to understand the wider issues such as shooting's place in the countryside and the pressures which face it, and its positive benefits in terms of recreation, conservation, employment and research.

Moral Aspects

First, however, you will have to sort out the moral aspects in your own mind, for although you are becoming involved in a process of managing a species and its habitat for its ultimate preservation, you are still taking a life. That process has evolved from a much older and more fundamental need, that mankind survived by hunting animals. From later eras cultivation has played a vital part in the supply of food. That, too, is manifestation of our role in the control of nature.

Our ability to do this, and produce an ordered society within nature, is fundamental to our existence. That we may not do it well at times, and that greed and ignorance produce injustices and waste, do not detract from the argument and sometimes obscure three fundamental things about it.

The first is that in nature death, which may frequently be violent, is necessary both to ensure the survival of the fittest for breeding purposes and as a source of food for other animals. In this context it is a fact of life, not a moral issue. The image of animals living to a contented retirement simply does not exist in the wild. The weak, ill or old, deprived of the instincts and ability to survive, provide the food for others to do so in a complex chain. These instincts of hunting and survival are inherent in humans, the dominant animal of that chain. They may be latent but cannot be totally

1988 was excellent on many grouse moors though fine warm days, such as this one at Middlesmoor in North Yorkshire, were as rare as they were welcome.

supressed and evidence of what happens if they are not channelled in a constructive way is all around us.

Second, from earliest times survival depended on a constant supply of meat. The understanding that this could only be guaranteed for as long as the quarry species itself survived and flourished is as old as hunting itself. This both imposes controls on the hunter – dictating how many and which animals should be killed and when – and the incentive to encourage the quarry to breed and to preserve its habitat, which in broad terms means conservation.

This leads to the third point which is that the close association developed over thousands of years between hunter, quarry, with their surroundings, and with other animals which share it, has provided man with an understanding of natural harmony and the wish to be part of it.

In modern terms these factors are evident in the written and unwritten laws which surround each country sport. The pattern of modern shooting, which

102

emerged from the need to provide food from wild sources, is based on culling the surplus after the breeding season which would perish anyway the following winter because of lack of food.

The system ensured a ready source of food, and left a strong and fit nucleus to breed the following season. Nowadays the shooter's assocation with his quarry motivates him to monitor numbers, carry out research, retain coverts and hedgerows and plant others, preserve wetland corners from drainage and cultivation, and keep ponds rather than fill them in.

As a result we still have quantities of grouse, wildfowl, woodcock, snipe, wild pheasants and partridges, not to say innumerable non-sporting birds and animals, so that Britain is a naturalist's as well as a field sportsman's paradise compared with other countries. Sometimes the press and public scorn Prince Philip's defence of shooting while promoting conservation, but field sportsmen understand his argument precisely and sympathise with his point of view.

However there is also an increasingly important field sports contribution in the modern context. Although in our predominantly urban lifestyle 'the urge to get out into the countryside' is a reminder of our association with nature, that very urban lifestyle also tends to encourage an artificial and unnatural view of it. This generates distorted and misguided views of our countryside and its wildlife. Because they have regular access to the countryside and understand how it works, field sports followers are in a position both to redress this balance and to monitor what is going on.

Country sports have a good record of recognising when things are going wrong and doing something about it. It was the shooting fraternity who discovered the damage that aldrin and dieldrin were doing to wildlife in the 1950s, which led to their withdrawal.

Fishermen monitor the quality of the waters and, in the Anglers' Cooperative Association, have an organisation whose sole role is to take action against polluters. It was the otterhunters who first warned of the effects modern farming were having on the otter population and stopped hunting them voluntarily. Harehunters have for long warned about farming's effects on hare populations. It has long been acknowledged, by government and conservation bodies, that grouse shooting preserves the heather moors. As the pressures on the countryside increase, from farming, recreation, access or whatever, field sports' role as a sheet anchor for conservation generally becomes more important.

Therefore killing animals does not on its own fulfill the hunting instinct. If it did little would survive. Conversely while conservation provides part of that fulfillment, the other part derives from the pursuit of quarry in its own surroundings and in a way which gives it every opportunity to escape.

Pursuit does not in itself worry an animal; fear or stress in this context is a human not an animal sensation. Animals do not share the human concept of death. The instincts of hunter and hunted are second nature to wild animals, and avoiding potential danger is part of the survival kit which cannot be judged in human terms. The kill is the necessary culmination of the hunt but, if the quarry escapes, the test of skill and challenge provided by the the chase may be just as fulfilling. So what is important in each field sport is how the pursuit is conducted. In the refined atmosphere of driven shooting it comes down to your conduct, the quality of your marksmanship and the choice of birds you shoot.

People talk about a 'sporting bird', but it is not easy to define. Basically it is a bird which has as much chance of escaping unscathed as you have of killing it cleanly. You do not shoot at low birds because it is unsafe, unchallenging, and renders the carcase inedible. Nor do you go shooting unless you are capable of consistently killing your quarry cleanly. The higher and faster the bird the greater the challenge and the greater its chance of eluding you. But there will be times when a bird is flying so high and fast that, although technically within range, you are not capable of killing it outright. The sporting ethic also requires you to acknowledge your limitations.

Marksmanship

The keys to enjoying shooting are marksmanship and how you fit in with the rest of the party, which will be dealt with in a later chapter. Marksmanship is vital, and there are few things more miserable than being out of your depth on a formal day's shooting. So before going shooting you must learn to shoot safely and accurately. Having done that you can improve with practice and gain confidence.

The traditional way of learning was to be put under the aegis of a gamekeeper at an early age. By accompanying him on his rounds you began to appreciate the ways of game and the natural history of the countryside. Then came carrying and handling a gun and learning how to care for it, and eventually even firing it at vermin. You might be allowed to attend a driven shoot as a spectator.

But only in the fullness of time, after years of absorbing game shooting in its entirety, did the great day come when you went on your first driven shoot, possibly on Boxing Day or a cocks-only day in January. It was a gradual and complete education, and lucky are those who can learn like that nowadays. For most of us the only way is through books and to go to a shooting school where you will be taught three things.

The first is about your gun, how it works and how to look after it. The second is how to carry it and use it safely. The safety aspect cannot be underlined enough, and you will not be taught how to shoot until your instructor is sure that you have

Contrasts in style: Charles Price, former US Ambassador, and his loader, William van Cutsem, on a Breckland shoot in Norfolk.

OPPOSITE *Traditionally the Gun is responsible for seeing that he and his loader are safe. In every one of these scenes the Gun is at fault, as well as (sometimes) the loader.*

Shooting straight is just a matter of pointing with the front hand, maintains former Olympic shot Michael Meggison at his Lancashire shooting ground.

understood the importance of safety and the practical steps of achieving it. Only then will you be introduced to moving targets. These will be in the form of clay pigeons. They are not ideal for game shots, because from the moment of release they tend to slow down whereas live game accelerates. Nevertheless they are good enough for you to be taught how to stand, mount your gun, swing, allow for lead and follow through.

Once you begin to master these, clays will be sent over you from a variety of heights, angles and speeds. Although driven game shooting involves quarry coming towards you, you will be surprised at the angles they appear from. You will also need to be able to shoot those which have crossed the line of Guns and which are going away.

Most good shooting schools will have traps which simulate pheasants, partridges, grouse, high birds and crossing birds so that by repetition and practice you will find that you hit them by reflex rather than consciously having to think about it. After a time you will realise another disadvantage about clay pigeons, which is that you know where they are coming from and when. Some shooting schools now have layouts where you walk down a lane and clays will come over from time to time and from various heights and angles without warning. If you hit these regularly you can be satisfied.

Learning to shoot is not difficult. Some people, endowed with superior co-ordination of hand and eye, are naturally good shots but most of us have to make do with application and practice. Each instructor has his own theories and methods. Providing you find that they work with you, it is wiser to avoid confusing the issue by learning others which invariably lead to your shooting worse rather than better. Many experienced Guns go back to shooting school each summer for a brush-up before the game season starts.

Although the Clay Pigeon Shooting Association has a scheme for instructors, game shooting has not. Nevertheless most country areas have a shooting school, and a local gunmaker or dealer will be able to recommend one if they do not have their own facilities. In addition BASC runs a Proficiency Award Scheme which provides a thorough grounding in shooting.

Sharing the Countryside

You will also need to be aware of the pressures which face your sport from opponents and, more particularly, from the many other recreations which also want to use the countryside. On at least two days every week during the season shooting must share the land with more than 350 packs of foxhounds, deer hounds, harriers and beagles. The Cobham Survey showed that of the 12 major outdoor activites, country sports was exceeded only by walking, football and swimming, and was more popular than golf, camping and caravanning, tennis, field studies, athletics and horse riding. In addition many who live in towns and who regard the countryside as their playground want a say in how it is run, even if they are neither entitled nor qualified.

Nevertheless however important shooting and other field sports are to rural areas they remain, like all pastimes, minority activities. How they survive into the twenty-first century depends on how they live with the others and adapt to changes. In addition shooting constantly faces new problems. Last year alone these included:

Major new legislation on ownership of sporting shotguns and rifles in the form of the Firearms (Amendment) Act.

New EEC laws which, if implemented in full, will stop shooting altogether except in specially permitted areas, will ban lead shot for clay shooting and in certain designated zones, impose bag limits, and introduce an 'environmental inspectorate'.

Another Common Market directive which would require all game meat sold in the UK to be inspected by vets within 24 hours of killing and to be plucked and drawn before being sold. Fortunately it looks as if Britain will be granted special immunity from these clauses.

Proposals which would allow an access free-for-all over grouse moors, and which would affect the birds' ability to breed and rear and thus affect grouse stocks.

Government changes to the planning laws (introduced with neither consultation with the shooting lobby nor vote in Parliament) reducing the number of days on which clay pigeon shooting can take place on land without planning permission from 28 days to 14. The government subsequently changed its mind and withdrew the changes after intense pressure and on learning that the proposed laws could not be implemented.

Implementation of the Wildlife and Countryside Act 1981 which will severely restrict the numbers of partridges released into the countryside.

Other problems include poaching, management agreements allowing sports to continue on Sites of Special Scientific Interest, paying VAT on sporting estates, an unfair rating system in Scotland, and how the Ministry of Agriculture's proposals for set-aside can benefit both shooting and wildlife.

Shooting must share the countryside with other field sports as well as other recreations. Here Captain Ronnie Wallace MFH visits Guns at the Mead's Farm shoot before going on to a New Year's Day meet.

The Hon. Richard Beaumont, Chairman of James Purdey & Sons, in the company's famous Long Room at its showrooms in South Audley Street, London. The Long Room Committee, formed there to counter the infamous 1973 Green Paper on firearms, eventually became the British Shooting Sports Council, the main representative body of all shooting sports.

IN DEFENCE

Field sports have a whole host of organisations, staffed with professionals in research, the countryside, public relations and politics, to resolve the problems. There are more than 30 bodies involved with shooting alone, from trade to muzzle loaders.

The British Shooting Sports Council (the successor to the old Long Room Committee founded in the famous Long Room at Purdey's, the gunmakers, to fight the then government's proposals to curb legitimate gun ownership in 1973) is the central organisation made up of representatives of the sport and trade bodies. It deals with the government and its departments, and had the task of introducing some sense into the Firearms (Amendment) Act last year. In fact it managed to wring 26 concessions from the government. It also managed to force it to form a Firearms Consultative Committee, comprised of members chosen by the Home Secretary and including representatives of shooting sports, to review the working of the firearms laws.

The main bodies concerned with protecting and advancing the interests of game shooting, and which rely entirely on the support of the shooting public, are:

The British Association for Shooting and Conservation, Marford Mill, Rossett, Clwyd LL12 OHL (telephone 0244 570881) is, with more than 100,000 members, the largest voluntary sporting body in Europe. Founded in 1908 as the Wildfowlers Association of Great Britain and Ireland, even after the war it was practically run from the boot of a car. It changed its name to its present one in 1981 to reflect that its influence extended far above the high water mark.

Now it promotes the interests of game and rough shooters, gun dog owners and stalkers as well as wildfowlers. Its remit covers politics at international, national and local levels, education, law, public relations, and research on firearms, quarry, habitat conservation and shooting. Because many wildfowl migrate it has strong links with international sporting and conservation bodies.

The British Field Sports Society, 59 Kennington Road, London SE1 7PZ (telephone 01-928 4742), which represents more than 72,000 members, is the umbrella body for all field sports. Its main strengths are its connections in parliaments in Westminster and Europe, its ability to fight laws which would affect field sports adversely and its strong public relations. In addition to fire-fighting the day-to-day threats to sports on a national basis, it has established a strong regional network through which it influences local issues effectively and promotes field sports. In these areas it works closely with the BASC.

The Game Conservancy, Fordingbridge, Hampshire SP6 1EF (telephone 0425 52381) emerged from the old Game Research Association and the Eley Game Advisory Station. It has a membership approaching 20,000 and is concerned with many aspects of research into game and the countryside, as well as implementing its findings. Projects its 36 research staff are currently investigating, at a cost of some £600,000 a year, cover the uplands, farmland, predation, wetlands, woodlands, wild and reared gamebirds, vermin and food among others. In addition its advisory department is in constant demand to advise shoots, and indeed has found its visits to estates increasing at the rate of 20% a year. It is also in demand abroad, and has a very high international standing.

It could be said that there is a measure of overlap between the roles of the BASC and BFSS, and there have been areas of friction in the past when one has come out with a different policy on a subject to the other. Nevertheless their strengths complement each other and on the main issues they provide a formidable combined front. The key is undoubtedly the BFSS's exceptional contacts with politicians and its understanding of parliamentary procedures.

The roles of the representative organisations are primarily to protect and promote, and ensure that shooting and other field sports live in harmony with each other and with other rural interests. Some field sports are not necessarily compatible even if, as a group, they have much in common. Nevertheless circumstances force them to co-operate with each other for survival, and goodwill must be created and fostered.

Although an integral part of the country scene, there was a danger in the past that opponents might succeed in isolating country sports from it. However much hard work behind the scenes in the last 15 years, and the efforts of bodies like the Standing Conference on Countryside Sports, have countered this.

A much stronger regional structure ensures that problems at a local level can be resolved effectively and that sportsmen, especially those who do not live in the countryside, are aware of their full obligations.

There is opposition to shooting and other field sports in varying degrees, in the same way that there is opposition of some sort or another to practically anything and everything. But although opponents claim that the public wants field sports stopped, a more accurate interpretation of their polls is that the public, always wary of those who want something which is perfectly legal banned, would prefer the status quo retained. An interesting recent example of this was the vote by members of the National Trust on a resolution to ban hunting over their land. Not only was the motion defeated; the fact that fewer than 76,000 of the Trust's 1.66 million members bothered to vote at all suggests that field sports are not the burning public issue that their opponents claim.

Whenever political parties threaten field sports, experienced politicians realise that to ban them would lose more votes than it would win. Nevertheless risks to country sports come from all directions, and it is only through resources and very hard work that they can continue. Anybody who follows a field sport regularly should support one or other of the organisations, and for the price of a brace of bottles of Scotch a year it is not much to ask.

The Cobham survey showed that the main reason for planting new woods was for game coverts. It is worth noting that the main reason for preserving many woods over the last two centuries was for foxhunting. The conifer wood shown here will also yield timber.

Contribution to Conservation

The third thing it may be helpful to know is shooting's contribution to the countryside in terms of recreation, economics and conservation. As we have already seen, Cobham estimated that the annual direct expendidure on country sports was £1 billion a year, and it put indirect expenditure at another £800,000,000 a year. That was more than was spent on air, bus and coach travel, radio and TV licences and rental, newspapers and on rail travel each year in Britain. It also vastly exceeded the amount spent on theatres, concerts, other shows and dances, and was more than 20 times greater than admissions to all spectator sports such as football matches and horse and dog racing. The expenditure provided direct full-time employment for 45,000 people, and indirectly for 43,000 more. It also contributed more than £200 million to the government in the form of rates, licenses and taxes. In 1980 shooting and stalking contributed a balance of trade surplus of £11.6 million. In terms of recreation and leisure, country sports provided up to 59 million activity days.

Although these figures were collated up to ten years ago and there has not been such a comprehensive survey since (although BASC and the Scottish Landowners' Federation are undertaking a new study in that country), they do provide a broad idea of what is involved. They may also be regarded as a base line for the current economic scale, because undoubtedly it will have increased since then. The Cobham figures were collated when the economy was in poor shape, inflation was rampant and an image of booming Britain no more than a pipe dream.

The boom, when it did arrive, also affected field sports. In the last ten years membership of BASC has increased from 60,000 to 100,000 members. Membership of the Game Conservancy and Clay Pigeon Shooting Association have doubled. The number of shotgun certificates has increased, and the amount of game released into our countryside is currently increasing at an estimated rate of 8% a year. The Game Conservancy's advisory service, which is responsible for helping estates to make the most of their shoots, reports an increase of 20% per annum in estate visits in each of the last three years. Such is the increased popularity of clay pigeon shooting that the CPSA has 100 clubs still awaiting inspection.

Cobham also presented evidence of the contribution of field sports to conservation. A Ministry of Agriculture survey in England and Wales during the 1970s found that more than half the farmers in the sample stated that country sports were either a primary or secondary reason for preserving wildlife on their land.

Cobham approached 100 occupiers of small woods of one hectare or less in Cambridgeshire, Norfolk, Hampshire, Durham and Powys which had received Countryside Commission grant aid for amenity tree planting between 1979–82. They were asked their main reasons both for conserving existing woodlands and for planting new ones. Cobham also approached 3700 members of the Timber Growers' Organisation with small woods of from one to ten hectares.

Of the nine reasons given, game coverts featured as the main one for planting new woods, and as second to beauty in the landscape as the reason for retaining existing ones. Of the nine different reasons they gave for either planting or retaining, game coverts came third behind landscape value and timber crop.

Nowadays few large farmers can afford to ignore the potential income from shooting in terms of annual rent and increased capital value. To this incentive can be added those of set-aside and the generous grants which are available for planting trees. These include:

a) The woodland grant scheme introduced in 1988 to replace the broadleaved woodland and forestry grant schemes. Administered by the Forestry Commission, it is for plantings covering an area greater than a quarter of an hectare where timber production is one of the main objectives.

b) The farm woodlands scheme, also introduced last year, and administered by the Ministry of Agriculture to encourage farmers to take from three to 40 hectares of agricultural land out of food production. The grants range from £30 to £190 per hectare for from 20 to 40 years depending on whether broadleaved trees, mixed woodlands or coppice are planted. Attractive though this sounds, farmers will have to be careful that their treatment of the soil when they grew crops on it, has not made it unsuitable for growing trees.

c) Additional grants for shelter belts and hedges provided by the Ministry of Agriculture.

d) Grants of up to 50% of costs for amenity tree planting on schemes not exceeding quarter of an hectare, available from the Countryside Commission.

e) Grants for small woodlands for conservation purposes, available from the Nature Conservancy Council.

f) Grants also available from local district councils.

On the 3000-acre Temple Estate in Wiltshire, where the Game Conservancy is creating a new wild pheasant and partridge shoot from scratch, up to 50% of all the costs of planting have come from grants.

ENTER THE GUNDOG

FOR many Guns a gundog is an inseparable and indispensible part of shooting. If there is a greater pleasure than watching a good gundog go about its work it is the fact that you have trained it and are handling it yourself.

For some Guns the enjoyment of gundog work becomes such that it eventually supercedes the enjoyment of shooting. Field trials, the competitive testing of gundogs under shooting conditions, are booming and the ranks of the pickers-up are also full of retired Guns who no longer shoot.

The dog is our oldest hunting ally, and the modern gundog part of a timeless tradition. That the Kennel Club lists 130 breed societies of 27 different gundog breeds reflects how quickly the gundog became established in our society, even if a large proportion of those bred nowadays are no more than household pets.

However nearly 140 field trial societies are also registered with the Kennel Club, which shows the strength of the sporting side. Field trials are more and more popular and are no longer regarded as merely an appendage of game shooting. Gundog work has become established as a sport in its own right. This has had the effect of increasing the numbers who want only to work gundogs joining up with shoots, thereby reducing the amount of work available for the Guns' own dogs. The pick-up at the end of a drive is a very slick operation, Guns and their dogs concentrating on birds near their pegs and picker-up teams mopping up the remainder. Certainly the operation must be done quickly so that Guns and beaters can move on to the next drive. This is especially so on commercially run shoots, which means that Guns have fewer opportunities to work their own dogs.

The present quality and popularity of gundog work have two other consequences. One is that good gundogs from working strains are expensive. The second is that a poorly trained or handled dog sticks out like a sore thumb; one of the main causes of a spoilt day's shooting is an unruly gundog, the owner becoming more demented as the dog becomes more unruly. So bear in mind that while you may be welcome,

A gundog's dream: Grouse moors in the distance, and coverts laid out for pheasants below. There are also partridges on this superb sporting estate at Middlesmoor, Yorkshire.

your gundog may not. If it is, it may play a restricted role. But none of this will stop the keen Gun from wanting to work a gundog.

For generations the gundog has been indispensible to hunt, flush and retrieve game from heavy cover or across water, and to find wounded game. This requires various qualities. A gundog hunts by scent, and must have a good nose; it must have courage, as well as the physical attributes, to face thick cover (or to retrieve a duck from the sea on a strong tide whipped up by icy, gale-force winds); it must persist and ignore temptations; and it must have a soft mouth so that quarry will not be damaged, even if struggling.

Each type of shooting (except clay pigeon!) has developed breeds to suit its own particular needs. As a result gundogs divide into four groups, retrievers, spaniels, pointers and setters, and the hunt/point/retrieve breeds favoured on the continent.

Retrievers

Retrievers, as their name suggests, are best suited for a driven game shoot where there is no need for them to hunt or flush game. The beaters, on the other hand, will require spaniels for working through cover.

The five breeds in the retriever group are the Labrador, Golden, Flatcoated, Curly-coated and Chesapeake Bay. The Labrador, either black or yellow (not to be confused with the Golden retriever) is the most popular on driven shoots, and because its excellent coat enables it to withstand wet and cold, it is also popular among wildfowlers.

Gundogs and their work: A golden retriever (top) and black labrador (right) retrieve cock pheasants.

David Jackson, well-known in the spaniel world, with his working cockers.

William Glencorse, a familiar face on Yorkshire's shooting scene, with two of his English springer spaniels.

Spaniels

Of the spaniel breeds the English and Welsh Springer, Cocker, Clumber, Irish Water, Sussex, and Field are seen on the shooting field with the English Springer by far the most popular. Its size and coat make it the ideal dog for facing all types of cover, however daunting, and its energy and determination equip it to hunt through it. Energy is the hallmark of the spaniel, and keeping that energy channelled and under control without dimming the dog's enthusiasm requires strong and sensitive handling and a good understanding.

In common with all the spaniel breeds, the Springer is the ideal rough-shooter's dog which will hunt game for you, flush it, mark its fall when you shoot, and retrieve it for you. In this context the wind of change in shooting does not bode well for the spaniels. The current commercial climate which encourages the up-grading of the good old fashioned rough shoots to something more commercially viable, may inhibit the breeds. The consequences of only doing part of the job – flushing birds which it will not retrieve when shot, or retrieving birds which it has neither flushed not marked – break a pattern which has been developed over generations.

Pointers and Setters

Before driven game shooting, the questing dogs reigned supreme (and commanded some high prices). There is no role in driven game shooting for pointers and setters, and although they are used for walking up partridges and pheasants, their main uses are to work heather for grouse. Nevertheless shooting over these dogs is one of the most rewarding types of shooting. Their purpose is to quarter ground in front of Guns and to indicate the presence of game, without flushing it, by 'pointing'. Guns can then move into position. There are five main breeds, the English pointer and the English, Irish, Irish Red and White and Gordon setters.

A pointer at work. When grouse are present the dog will remain motionless on point while the Guns prepare, and until the order to flush is given.

The English setter: Field trial winner Jack of Sharnberry at work.

The HPRs

Similarly there is no recognised role in driven game shooting for the HPR breeds, which have gained some popularity since the last war. In essence they are pointers which also retrieve, and although the breeds most commonly found in this country come from far-flung origins in Europe, they are basically pointers which can retrieve with particular reference to local conditions.

A Weimeraner, one of the continental hunt, point and retrieve breeds.

The most popular HPR breeds seen in this country are the German shorthaired pointer, German wirehaired pointer, the Large Munsterlander, Vizsla, and Weimeraner. The Brittany, a consequence of those days when Englishmen went partridge shooting in Brittany and crossed setters with the local spaniel, and the Spinone, have only recently got a toehold in this country. The Weimeraner is the biggest in the group because it was expected to combine the role of guard dog with an ability to face boar. The German wirehaired pointer's coat can withstand heavy cover and cold. The only Italian Spinone I have seen working, on the sandy soil of Suffolk, was a wizard in dry conditions where other gundogs could make little of them.

Finding Your Dog

A day's shooting can be spoiled for everyone by an unruly gundog. If you decide to own a gundog, you owe it to your fellow sportsmen (and the dog) to train and handle it properly. Bad news travels surprisingly quickly in the shooting fraternity, and invitations to shoot usually dry up for one of two reasons. Either your marksmanship is doubtful and unsafe, or your four-legged companion is a liability.

Once you have chosen what breed of gundog you want, there are various ways of going about obtaining one. You can either buy a puppy and train it yourself or send it off to be trained, you can buy a partially-trained young dog, or you can buy a fully-trained gundog. There is a great deal of personal satisfaction in choosing your own puppy – or even breeding your own – and seeing it subsequently perform well on the shooting field. But you will need a lot of experience both of shooting and gundog breeding.

Worker or House Mutt

Gundogs provide a whole new dimension to shooting, and the keener the Gun, the more likelihood he will sooner or later own one. Nevertheless a gundog is a major undertaking, and the addition of one to your household will have major consequences.

If you do decide to get one, you will have to make three decisions. The first is to choose the right breed for your requirements, and before you can do that you must decide what type of shooting you prefer.

The second is whether you want a gundog or a household pet. In serious working gundog circles the two do not mix: the pleasures and comforts of family household life distract from the disciplines and fitness needed for work at the highest levels. You may not want a gundog to work at the highest levels, and may prefer less demanding standards and a dog which fits in with the family. It is achievable if you are realistic, accept certain limitations of performance when you go out shooting, and ensure that you remind your dog regularly what it is there for.

The third is how you train your gundog, either doing it yourself or sending it off to a good trainer. If you decide to undertake the training you must make sure that you have the time, patience and aptitude. A mistake at the initial stages will be difficult to put right, but although there may appear to be many pitfalls, don't let them put you off.

Good gundogs are a result of physique, instinct, temperament and training among other things, and when you select a puppy you will need to know it has more than a fair chance of possessing the first three. You would be lucky to find sufficient instinct to rekindle from a strain which produces good household pets where the will as well as the instinct have become redundant.

Time spent on research is not wasted. You will need the offspring of working ancestry. That means examining pedigrees and working records, and talking to people. The gundog world is close-knit, and nobody wants to earn a reputation for selling poor dogs. Most people who sell puppies are only too willing to provide evidence of a working ancestry, especially if it contains a Field Trial Champion or two. Field trial results will tell you a lot.

Always be careful, however, to find out if there are either congenital weaknesses such as progressive retinal atrophy, retinal dysplasia or hip dysplasia (it is possible to find strains free of them), or vices. It is no use paying a lot of money for a dog only to discover that it either whines or has a hard mouth and that a parent did as well.

Do not hesitate to seek advice from those who work gundogs or from professional trainers – there are some 50 well-known ones dotted around the countryside, and many more who keep smaller establishments. Gamekeepers are often a good source of contacts, but remember that although they have wide practical experience of gundogs, it is not their prime role in life.

Gundogs are often advertised in the sporting press. Alternatively a gundog trainer will find either a suitable puppy or fully trained dog for you. Professional trainers handle many dogs which, while not up to the high standards required for top competitive field trial work, would be more than adequate for the shooting field.

Deep Wallet

You must be prepared to to pay for a good gundog. Trainers never cease to comment that shooting people are happy to spend large sums on guns, accessories, clothes and their sport, but expect not to have to pay highly for a gundog. There is no cutting corners with a gundog in either time or money.

Some experts say that the best time to take a pup from the litter is no later than seven weeks, when it will transfer its link with its mother to its new owner easily and before it becomes a member of the pack. At that stage you would expect to have to pay between £100 and £150, but a glance through the classified advertisements in the current sporting press reveals the following: a two and a half year old English Springer spaniel bitch, with field trial awards, for £600; a trained black Labrador dog for £550; a nine-month old black Labrador dog, £275; Labrador puppies by a field trial winner, £125; GSP puppies for £110; an 11-month old German Wirehaired pointer ready to train on for £300; a 20-month old part-trained Brittany for £200, a fully trained four year old working Cocker spaniel bitch for £425; and a 16-month old English Springer bitch, basic training completed, for £150.

The Training Factor

The point to emerge from all this is that to the inherent value of the instinct must be added the value of training. By the time you start even the most basic training, at about eight months, you will probaly have spent again the cost of the pup. Training it yourself will take time, patience and care, strict routine and the right conditions.

It is no use trying to make a go of it if your only training ground is Clapham Common with all its distractions, or if the dog has become accustomed to sleeping on one of the children's beds. If you make a mistake you may have to send the dog off to a professional to sort out anyway, and by then it could be too late.

Off to Kennels

If you decide not to train the dog yourself, the financial stakes rise. The minimum time a professional trainer needs on the average dog is six months. For some it will be longer, and it will be difficult for him to charge anything less than £30 a week to care for your dog and train it. So by the time it is basically trained, and even before it has been introduced to the shooting field properly, the better part of £1000 may have been spent.

If you do have it trained by a professional, you must take care that the stage when it leaves the trainer and comes under your control is handled with care and sensitivity. You will also have to learn how to handle it, and before that you will have to learn how to communicate with it.

125

One of John Halstead's dogs demonstrates a bold entry into water.

Field trial champion Haretor Shadow of Drakeshead looks suitably bored in the rabbit pen. In time the young yellow labrador will also become immune to rabbits.

In fact many reputable trainers regard the transition of gundog to owner as so important that they will spend a session or two with both of them to ensure that the lines of communication are clear. Make the most of these sessions. They will teach you not only how to get your gundog to do something when you want it to, but how to stop it successfully when you don't – the last thing a host wants to see (or hear) in the middle of a drive is a Gun bellowing vainly at his dog as it sets off in hot pursuit of a runner. Apart from the distraction, Guns are there to shoot.

The more you can understand of its character, capabilities, physical strengths and limitations and moods the more rewarding you and your dog will find each other's company. These can be learned as you gradually introduce your dog to the shooting field and gain in confidence. It is a gradual process and cannot be hurried. But it is well worth the time and money, because as the seasons go by you will have much enjoyment. You will think twice about going shooting without your dog, and in the end you may even find that it is the gun you leave behind.

Your Gundog on a Shoot

When the invitation to a day's driven shooting does come, you will need to find out if your dog is welcome too. However it would be wise to put some thought to the matter even before you ask. You, or to be more correct your dog, may be able to get away with some things on your syndicate where you have, after all, paid and hence have some say. But when you are invited to someone else's shoot the rules change.

For instance you should not even consider taking it if you have doubts about controlling it, if it has a vice – fights, runs in, whines, yaps, has a hard mouth, is not steady to fur, pinches other Gun's birds, disputes the ownership of birds with other dogs – or if you have a bitch in season.

If your dog is young and comparatively inexperienced, you may prefer not to ask so as not to embarrass your host by his refusal. If you do ask, explain the situation. Even if your dog is experienced he may say no because he has delegated the task to a team of pickers-up and does not want his schedule upset, although on most shoots the more dogs there are to pick up the quicker the operation is finished.

If permission is granted, keep the dog under constant control. Try and give it a good run before arrival just to take the edge off. Ensure that it does not spoil the enjoyment of others, does not chase livestock, or wander into coverts between drives. Always carry a lead in case you have to cross roads. But make sure that it is a slip lead; never allow your dog to work in a collar in case it gets hung up by it on wire or under water. Make sure that you take the lead off in the car so it cannot become hung up there, either. If you are worried about your dog not staying beside you during a drive, obtain a corkscrew spike so that it can be secured to the ground.

Under no circumstances tie your dog to yourself during a drive; there have been some horrifying accidents.

At the end of each drive ensure that your dog picks only the birds that you have shot. This puts the onus on you to mark and count them. However neighbouring Guns may well welcome help from your dog. But do not assume it, and do not let your dog pick someone else's bird unless you have asked first. He may want his own dog to retrieve it.

If you are on the boundary of the shoot, don't allow your dog to retrieve from the other side of it unless you have been allowed to. Try not to upset your host's

Gun and loader concentrate on approaching birds while the gundogs do what they are supposed to do, mark fallen game. The net has been placed permanently in the hedge to prevent partridges from flying through the gap.

schedule by keeping him and other Guns waiting; keep an eye on him and, if he has a team of pickers-up, inform them of any bird you have failed to retrieve and leave it to them.

You won't need reminding always to ensure the well-being of your dog. Cuts and sprains, and anything more serious, will become obvious during the day. And the more you get to know your dog the more you will be able to 'feel' if it is well within itself. If it loses its zest for working you will need to take veterinary or professional advice.

More difficult to recognise is how tired your dog is, especially after a hard morning at the start of the season before it has had a chance to become fully fit, and its enthusiasm for work may mask tiredness. There is nothing more daunting for a young inexperienced dog than to ask too much of it. Many handlers (and the same goes for riders of young horses in the hunting field) stop them working when they still have enough energy to enjoy themselves so that they will look forward eagerly to the next time. If in doubt, leave your dog in the car after lunch (don't forget to put the windows down an inch or two to allow in fresh air).

After shooting look after your dog before you look after yourself. Before putting your dog back into the car dry it off with a towel or sack, and leave it something dry to lie on. You can now buy dog sacks into which you can zip your dog after a day's shooting so that it will remain warm and get dry. It also keeps the inside of your car cleaner. Provide it with clean water and, if you have far to go, some food. When you get home check that it is not suffering any after-effects, and no cuts or thorns.

WHERE TO SHOOT

I F you do not own or lease a shoot, or are not one of those witty and gracious marksmen who always get invited, there are only two main ways to obtain regular shooting. One is to join a syndicate, the other to rent sport by the day.

Choosing a Syndicate

Syndicates grew from a need among landowners to spread the costs of their own sport. Some of these costs were astronomical, a legacy from the days before the first world war, and were further aggravated by the agricultural depression in the years following it. Estates were faced with the prospect of either visiting Guns helping to pay, or stopping altogether. As a result syndicates increased in various forms. Some were formed by the landowner who retained the sporting rights. Some sold the sporting rights over their land, some leased them and others let out days.

Nowadays, with ever-rising costs, there is a trend for neighbouring private shoots to band together, get some outside Guns in to help share the costs and pool the sport. It may mean an owner no longer having absolute control of the shooting, but there are compensations in terms of a larger shoot and scope for improvement of sport as well as costs. But whatever its shape, the syndicate was for years about the only way for a Gun who did not own a shoot to have his own sport regularly, and for an owner to enjoy his asset without feeling the shadow of the bank manager looking over his shoulder.

There are many advantages in belonging to a syndicate. You can choose a convenient one in terms of distance, cost and frequency. If you choose the right one (and they choose you) you will be among kindred spirits in familiar surroundings. You will get to know the lie of the land, how the birds fly and the pattern of the day. There can also be a greater sense of involvement in how the shoot is run.

With the ease of transport these days there is a much wider choice than there used to be. If you live in the countryside, to find out what is available it is usually only a matter of sounding out through the bush telegraph. If you live in a town, however, it might be worth looking in the classified advertisements of the sporting press (*The Field*, *Shooting Times* or *Countrysport*), or approaching a reputable sporting agent.

Some sporting agents are adjuncts to local estate agents, and others are independent, but the good ones share the virtue of having both extensive intelligence networks and the ability to fit square pegs into square holes.

Joining the right syndicate is a matter of trial and error to some extent, and the sizing up is a two-way business. A syndicate will want to know as much about you, and whether or not you are an all-round good-egg as well as a safe shot, as you will about them. You will need to know about the other Guns, the layout of the shoot, about the gamekeeper, and you will want to inspect the game book in detail to make sure that you know what you are joining.

You may also want to look at the relationship between shoot and estate owner. The success of any shoot often depends on how well it integrates with other estate considerations like farming and forestry. Neither, especially modern farming methods, need be compatible with shooting but both can be. The planting of crops in strategic places as either food or holding cover can make all the difference. This co-operation and integration is well worthwhile because it reflects both in the bag and in the rental and capital values of land. Check also the topography and layout of the shoot – on the lie of the land and the placing of the coverts, among other things, will depend the quality of the shoot. Checking the background takes time, but as the commitment may be for a lifetime, it is not something to rush.

The cost of shooting, whether taken by the season or the day, is based on the cost of each bird shot, and excludes those which fly on unscathed. The Game Conservancy estimates that the average for a pheasant or partridge is £14–£15. Multiply that by the the average of the annual bag over several recent seasons and you will come to an approximate figure. There may also be additional factors. Shoots close to big cities are more expensive than those which require travel. Shooting mid-week is usually cheaper than on a Saturday.

Through the pages of the sporting press last season, advertisements sought Guns for 12 Thursdays on a 4,000-acre shoot near Newmarket, on which 6,000 birds had been released, for £2,900. Another for 14 Saturdays in the midlands over 3,000 acres, again 6,000 birds released, sought Guns for £3,500.

A re-formed Sussex pheasant shoot with 1,200 birds released was seeking Guns for £800 for the season; another in Wiltshire, shooting pheasants and duck on Saturdays, was priced at £450; and a Norfolk estate was offering eight Fridays shooting pheasants and partridges for £1,840. An enterprising Nothumberland estate offered 15 days – one day walked-up grouse, six days walked-up mixed

PREVIOUS PAGE *An unusually large and early pack of grouse approaches the butts. The Gun watches how his neighbours perform, while the well-trained loader keeps an eye on the other flank.*

Will the birds fly properly? This one, high over Peter Kane at Chilcomb's drive by 'The Square', certainly did, and so did several hundred more.

shooting, and eight days driven pheasant shooting followed by duck flighting for £1,850.

So there is plenty of choice. The main difficulty is to reconcile the depth of your pocket with how often you can go shooting, where, that you like your fellow Guns and, very important, that the shooting is of the quality and quantity that suits you.

The secret is to be able to assess your own ability accurately. You won't want to shoot low-flying birds with the lead whistling round your ears, and there is nothing more confidence-sapping than continually missing birds which are too high for you to kill consistently.

Flying Syndicates

Nevertheless running a shoot does have its worries, and belonging to a syndicate means that you have to share them. Will the reared birds fly properly? Will Joe Bloggins keep his wretched dog under control? Will the storm have damaged the coverts? Will the birds have a nervous breakdown if the local pack of hounds runs through the coverts? Have the poachers stitched you up? Will the beaters turn up? Are the pickers-up any good? You go shooting to get away from your worries, not to add to them.

One noticeable development in recent years is what might be termed the Flying Syndicate, a syndicate which has given up actually running a shoot, and rents sport by the day. They go where and when they please, simply book, turn up and shoot and enjoy themselves, and settle-up later. Worry is kept to a minimum.

Look in the sporting press nowadays and you will see how the market for shooting is changing. The majority of advertisements now offer sport by the day. That does not signify the demise of the syndicate shoot. Far from it. The syndicate remains the backbone of the sport. What it does indicate is both the growth of shooting's popularity, and how it has adapted itself to the competitive recreation and entertainment markets. The difference between these markets may appear slight, but it has a profound effect on both the quality of sport offered and shooting's public image.

Sport by the Day

In addition to the Flying Syndicate there are many Guns, or groups of Guns, taking advantage of two interconnecting trends. Nowadays many established shoots rent days to help cover costs rather than having paying syndicate Guns. Also there are few farmers with suitable land who can afford to ignore the sporting potential of their land, especially with the government's policy of set-aside and generous grants to plant woods. The result, apart from the demise of the good old fashioned rough

In 1988 grouse shooting rents ranged from £45 to £75 per brace. Here Christopher Shepherd is the Gun, Steve Lupton the loader.

shoot, is that there is currently a surplus of shooting. Many sporting agents report that there are some bargain days to be had.

The second trend is that because a day's shooting is suitable for business entertaining, the packaging and marketing have become highly sophisticated. In this market, where business is often generated by word of mouth and by parties returning year after year, a shoot cannot afford things to go wrong. If they do, regardless of the circumstances (and in shooting one is dealing with many imponderables of nature), a hard-nosed businessman will simply take his custom elsewhere. As a result you know precisely what you are going to get – the number of birds anticipated, their quality, how detailed the arrangements are from the moment you arrive, the matter of refreshments – and how much it is going to cost.

Many shoots also have arrangements with local hotels which, because the main holiday season is over, are keen to offer good-value packages of bed, breakfast and dinner. Indeed there are many hotels which, to keep their rooms filled during the winter, have taken the initiative and organise shooting days for their guests.

These trends have provided Guns with a far wider choice. Instead of taking regular days on one shoot throughout the season, they seek pastures new, take their other halves, and treat it as a weekend break or short holiday. It is not all plain sailing, and you will need to do your homework. While the old-established shoots have had time to get their acts together, newer shoots need time to mature, so to speak. Standards on a few commercial shoots can be decidedly patchy, to say the least.

Be careful taking days early in a season. There may be more birds about, but if there is a lot of leaf still on the tree and the undergrowth has not died back, birds are more difficult to flush. Nor will they learn to fly well until they have been over the Guns once or twice.

In addition to the bag, the logistics – the swift and efficient transporting of Guns between drives, the frequency with which birds are flushed and how well they fly over Guns, the quality of refreshments, the cheerfulness and helpfulness of staff – will reflect in the costs as well as in the degree of enjoyment.

Few commercial shoots can afford to charge less than the £15 average it costs to put each bird in the bag, although some may be able to because of other factors of estate management. However most shoots which rear and release birds can organise a day so that the size of the bag can be predicted, so you will know what to expect.

Before last season sporting agents reported that the best pheasant shooting would cost £22 per bird, with the average somewhere between £15 and £20. For grouse the figure was from £45 to £75 per brace. Multiply these figures by the bag and you will have your shooting costs. Agents say that they seldom have difficulty in letting their best days – happy are those shoot owners who have the same parties returning season after season.

One way to show what is on offer is to examine what happened on three shoots last season. They have been chosen because of their geographical differences, how they are run, and because they have a high return rate of satisfied customers.

One is a west-country hotel, best known for its game fishing, but which also arranges pheasant, woodcock and duck shooting. It is particularly well-known for the four-day snipe shoots it arranges between the end of November and the end of January.

Snipe are the most difficult targets whether driven or walked-up, and many a shooting reputation has been tarnished by these elusive birds. The first problem is to find them. You can walk over field after field, all appearing to be ideal habitat, before you find one. But that is not necessary, for the secret is the local intelligence network. In this case the parties are organised by a local farmer who knows both the lie of the land and everybody who lives on it. He can therefore take Guns immediately to where there is a likelihood of birds, and he is seldom wrong.

Once found, though, there are other challenges. Snipe are wary and easily disturbed, sometimes getting up either out of shot or before the Guns have had time to get into position. Stealth is essential. There is a knack to organising a successful snipe drive. Guns are usually placed behind a hedge. Because snipe tend to fly low initially after being put up, the Guns are sometimes asked to turn the backs to the beaters and to shoot the birds going away. There may be between eight and fifteen drives per day, depending on whether or not the birds are in, and drives can vary between wisps of a few to hundreds.

The shoots last from Monday to Thursday with parties of up to ten Guns. Guns are asked to arrive in time for dinner and a briefing on the Sunday night. The cost per Gun of £485 (which includes VAT) covers four days shooting and transport, all

Waiting for snipe: Some Guns prefer to shoot them only going away.

meals, and five nights accommodation with a private bath or shower room. Non-shooting partners pay £235.

The second example is on a large privately-owned estate on undulating country in Warwickshire, with the period house set on a hill overlooking the countryside. Shooting in such countryside, and having lunch in the impressive surroundings of the family home, add to the enjoyment of a well-organised day.

The estate offers 21 shooting days from mid-October to the first week in January. Two mixed pheasant and partridge days, with an anticipated bag of 100 head for £1,000 (plus VAT) for eight Guns, start the season. Pheasant days range from an anticipated bag of 130 head for £1,625 plus VAT for eight Guns, to 400 pheasant days for £5,600 plus VAT. For each Gun it will therefore cost between £233 for the 130-pheasant day to £805 for the 400 pheasant day when VAT has been added. This works out at between £12.50 and £14 per pheasant, which is extremely competitive. Non shooting guests are welcome for an additional £13.80 to cover the cost of lunch.

The third example is a large, professional operation which offers grouse, partridge and pheasant shooting over 12,000 acres of estates in south-east Scotland. The season starts on 19 August with walked-up grouse shooting at £110 per Gun per day, exclusive of VAT.

As a contrast the best days on the low ground, which produce over 400 head of pheasant and partridge, would cost £450 per Gun excluding VAT. As an inbetween there are four-day shoots in November and December, a mixture of walking up and driving, with an expected bag of 100 head a day at a cost of £120 per Gun per day.

12

BEHIND THE SCENES

'IN personal appearance he would be a tall man were it not that he has contracted a slight stoop in the passage of years, not from weakness or decay of nature, but because men who walk much lean forward somewhat, which has a tendency to round the shoulders. The weight of the gun, and often of a heavy gamebag dragging downwards, has increased this defect of his figure and, as is usual after a certain age, even with those who lead a temperate life, he begins to show signs of corpulency.

'But these shortcomings only slightly detract from the manliness of his appearance, and in youth it is easy to see that he must have been an athlete. There is still plenty of power in the long sinewy arms, brown hands, and bull neck and intense vital energy in the bright blue eye. He is an ash-tree man, as a certain famous writer would say; hard, tough, unconquerable by wind or weather, fearless of his fellows, yielding but by slow and imperceptable degress to the work of time.

'His neck has become the colour of mahogany; sun and tempest have left their indelible marks upon his face; and he speaks from the depths of his broad chest, as men do who talk much in the open air, shouting across the fields and through the copses. There is a solidity in his very footstep, and he stands like an oak. He meets your eye full and unshirkingly, yet without insolence; not as the labourers do, who either stare with sullen ill-will or look on the earth. In brief, freedom and constant contact with nature have made him every inch a man; and here in this nineteenth century of civilised effeminacy may be seen some relic of what men were in the old feudal days when they dwelt practically in the woods . . .

'Perfectly civil to everyone, and with a willing manner towards his master and his master's guests, he has a wonderful knack of getting his own way. Whatever the great house may propose in the shooting line, the keeper is pretty certain to dispose of in the end as he pleases; for he has a voluble "silver" tongue and is full of objections, reasons, excuses, suggestions, all delivered with a deprecatory air of superior knowledge . . .'

The gamekeeper at work: Jack Blude, head 'keeper at Leighton Hall in Lancashire, blows his horn to signal the start of a drive.

Richard Jefferies' classic description of the gamekeeper still rings true since it first appeared in *The Gamekeeper at Home* in 1878. The pressures and demands may be different, but the gamekeeper remains the central figure on the shoot to whom everyone involved, including the owner, usually defers. He is the stage manager, co-ordinating the game, the people and the dogs. To fulfill this role he must have the same qualities of toughness, independence, self-reliance, common sense and diplomacy Jefferies so observantly described.

The Cobham Survey put the number of full and part-time gamekeepers in Britain at 5,000, reflecting one of the major changes among the 'keepers ranks. The days when many shoots had a head 'keeper, with beat keepers and underkeepers, have gone. In these days of do-it-yourself shoots it is as likely to be a part-timer or an amateur.

But then this merely reflects the social revolution. Before the first world war the estate was employer and, in its paternalistic way, looked after those who lived on it. Son succeeded father as gamekeeper as son succeeded father in the big house. The job was in the blood so to speak. Jefferies' reference to the 'relic' from feudal times acknowledges that the gamekeeper's inheritance precedes the advent of shooting.

Nowadays gamekeepers come from a variety of backgrounds, urban as well as rural. It is perhaps a pity that some of the old, thorough ways of doing things have gone, and that some of the modern attitudes are not those of the traditional countryman.

But shooting has benefitted from fresh and enquiring minds and unbiased attitudes. The modern gamekeeper has a far broader perception of shooting, capable of coping with its greater external pressures, than his predecessor. Instead of learning exclusively from others, some modern gamekeepers also learn much in the classroom. The courses offered by the Hampshire College of Agriculture at Sparsholt, for instance, which has been in the forefront of educating gamekeepers, fully recognise the wider range of skills which will be needed.

In 1986 it started a National Diploma course in game, wildlife and habitat management, with two years in the classroom and a year's practical work on estates in the UK and America. As well as gamekeeping the course covers woodland management, conservation, ecology and deer management, machinery maintenance, finance and legal matters, and farm liaison. In addition both the Game Conservancy and the BASC run courses for both amateur and professional keepers which cover a wide range of subjects, from habitat conservation to predator control.

Shoots do not now have the large staffs they used to and 'keepers must do much of the work themselves, very often alone and unsupervised. To help them there is an array of modern methods and equipment. A 'keeper must be as conversant with using and servicing computers, communication systems, electronic surveillance, and four-wheel transport as he is with his poults or his accounts.

The modern gamekeeper can turn to the Game Conservancy for tried and tested expertise on a whole range of practical aspects including providing the correct cover, food and care for young birds, and vermin control. It has an advisory service, and will visit his shoot to provide an independent assessment of how it might be improved. The research it is doing now will eventually lead to more relevant information.

But however well the modern gamekeeper is educated, equipped and advised, the priorities have not changed. He is there to provide sport. If he fails, for whatever reason, he takes the responsibility. Even if the owner's demands are unreasonable, in this unfair world the gamekeeper takes the blame. After all, of all relationships between landowner and staff which have been forged over the years, the gamekeeper has always had a privileged position and direct access to his governor.

The gamekeeper's job falls into five main categories: providing food and cover to allow his gamebirds to breed and prosper; protecting them by controlling avian and ground vermin; on lowland shoots rearing and releasing birds to supplement the wild stocks; organising each day's shooting; protecting his stocks from poachers. To this can be added public relations at a sensitive time for field sports. The gamekeeper is at the hub of country life. He must know what is going on around him and is at the centre of a sophisticated intelligence system. This is as useful to the general field sports movement in the protection of their interests as it is to the local police in combatting poaching. The gamekeeper is in the ideal position to forge good relations with the local huntsmen, farmers, neighbouring keepers and everybody else on local farms and estates.

Harry Green, part-time 'keeper at Barnacre, also acts as a picker-up with his golden retrievers.

In everthing he undertakes it is important for a gamekeeper to maintain a balance. If he can it produces two desireable qualities in shooting. One is the balance between wild and reared birds so that the quality of the shoot is maintained. The other is the quality of the habitat so that other species, especially songbirds, benefit. On one recent Game Conservancy survey, woodland rides created especially for shooting had attracted 19 different species and over 40 times as many butterflies. The conservation aspects of shooting are as important to the sport and its image as they are to the countryside.

One of the dangers of the commercialisation of shooting is that the quality of sport is sacrificed to the numbers killed. The gamekeeper comes under pressure simply to produce large quantities of birds – the fact that there may be insufficient cover to hold them on the ground or to fly to is sometimes even disregarded.

In producing the large numbers required the 'keeper may be forced to neglect other important duties, such as vermin control or maintaining cover. Add these to the consequences of large bags of poorly presented reared pheasants, and the image of shooting suffers accordingly. Positive is positive in shooting; negative is very negative indeed.

The gamekeeper's year does not stop. At the end of one shooting season he must think of the next. By the time he has cleaned and scrubbed his equipment, prepared his pens, and done his vermin control, the wild birds will be hatching or he will be coping with reared stock. From the moment his charges come under his control to the moment they finally leave the release pens, his job will be very demanding. Because the birds are concentrated they are vulnerable to disease, weather, predation or poaching. And then it is the next shooting season again.

Game Rearing

To help him the gamekeeper can buy in stock from game farmers. Some gamekeepers produce their own eggs by catching up pheasants and incubating their eggs artificially. Others, however, either buy in eggs, day-old chicks or older poults depending on their circumstances. There are advantages of cost, time or manpower in each.

There are some 50 recognised game farmers in Britain, spread through most counties, who are members of the Game Farmers' Association. In addition there are numerous shoots which rear their own birds and sell off the surplus. Figures for the amount of game released each year are hazy, but the Game Conservancy thinks that it is 20–25 million pheasants and partridges a year. Judging from information provided by game feed suppliers and other sources, they think that it has been increasing at the rate of 8% for the last three years.

OPPOSITE *Tunnel traps, in the right place, do the 'keeper's job for him. They must, by law, be inspected daily. Here Hugh van Cutsem checks one on his Norfolk Breckland shoot at Hilborough.*
FAR RIGHT *However many birds are released, however well fed they are, and however dry and warm their coverts, they will not survive – or will not even be born (below) – if vermin go unchecked.*

Vermin Control

However many birds are released, however well fed they are, and however dry and warm their coverts, they will not survive if the vermin go unchecked. Vermin divide into two groups. Ground vermin include foxes, rats, stoats and weasels, mink, feral cats and grey squirrels. Among the birds are the corvids and some gulls, particularly the black-backed.

Gamebird stocks will also suffer to an extent from the raptors and owls, and gamekeepers are only just beginning to get over the poor image they used to have for the indiscriminate slaughter of the owls, hawks and falcons which are now protected by the Wildlife and Countryside Act.

The traditional ways to control vermin are shooting, snaring, trapping and poisoning. Shooting is largely a question of opportunity, and few gamekeepers leave their guns behind on their rounds. Snaring, effective and safe for the unintended in the right hands, is under pressure from certain lobbies. Poisons are obviously restricted, but certain legally prescribed ones, such as proprietary brands of rat poison, can be very effective. There are also proprietary brands of both cage and tunnel traps which, in the right place, do the gamekeeper's job for him.

Poaching

The gamekeeper can also call for help against poachers. The popular image of the poacher outwitting the squire and his 'keeper to get something for the pot still persists. But in reality poaching is done by well-organised, efficient and ruthless urban gangs which make the most of the motorways. Game worth thousands of pounds is poached every year, and this says nothing of the waste, damage or cruelty inflicted.

Many police forces, landowners and gamekeepers now co-operate closely and this rural intelligence network is beginning to prove effective. It has also helped by telling 'keepers what they can and cannot do in law, and providing practical advice on how to apprehend poachers. There are poacherwatch schemes. Sporting bodies frequently organise courses and conferences.

Modern technology also helps. Most shoots are now equipped with walkie-talkies and various alarm systems. Some have also installed in their coverts a series of detectors, which either by breaking beams or heat detection relay intrusion to a central console. Quite apart from not having to be outdoors all hours of the night, it also means that the gamekeeper need not worry about being in the wrong place at the wrong time.

Game Dealer

The gamekeeper may also use a game dealer to dispose of the bag. Each weekend during the pheasant shooting season there may be anything up to a million carcases. A brace will go to every Gun, and some are given away. Even so that leaves vast numbers of birds coming onto the market.

Game may only be sold by someone with a game licence, and then only to a licenced game dealer (there is a Game Dealers' Association). A gamekeepers' licence, authorising him to kill game, allows a gamekeeper to dispose of a shoot's game through a licensed dealer providing he has written permission from his employer. Under the Game Act 1831 and Game Licences Act 1860 a game dealer needs two licenses, one from his council and another from his post office. If you buy game from someone who is not a licensed game dealer (such as a few extra birds from your host) you are in fact liable to a fine.

The sale of birds is one way in which a shoot can help to offset costs, and vast numbers of grouse, pheasants, partridges, pigeons and hares are sold onto the continent. They will fetch the market price, which is subject to fluctuation. If, for instance, there is a sudden influx through the European capitals of plucked and dressed pheasants from Hungary, it will affect the price of the bag on a shoot in

Wiltshire. Last season prices paid to British shoots were as low as £1.50 per brace – half what they were a few years ago – even if butchers were selling them at £6 a brace plucked and dressed.

Beaters

The gamekeeper also needs the services of beaters and pickers-up. In the days of large and labour-intensive estates, beaters came from the estate staff.

Now they come voluntarily and from across the social scale, from farm labourers, local townees wanting a day in the country, Guns' sons keen for experience, lads keen to get a foothold into shooting, someone who wants to work their dog; all attracted by the thought of a day out in the countryside for a tenner, a can of beer and a loaded bun, a dinner and possibly a day's shooting at the end of the season.

The art of beating is not as straightforward as it may seem. Having built up a team – which may be anything up to a dozen or more on a pheasant shoot – 'keepers try to change them as little as possible and hence becoming a beater in some areas may not be easy. Being part of the team, however, requires hard work and concentration.

Whether through heather on the hills, across stubble for partridges, a muddy field of kale, or thick woodland cover for pheasants, the going for beaters is never easy.

Sledmere's beaters' transport is drier and less draughty than most. Guns should never forget to appreciate beaters' efforts. Not only is it good manners, but an appreciated beater is a better beater.

The straight line must be maintained through thick and thin, both to ensure that game does not slip back and for safety, and proceed at a pace which will give the dogs time to work the ground. The art is to get birds to flush in a steady stream, not in one great uprising at the end of a drive. So the beater must keep one eye on the 'keeper and the line, and the other on beating out the cover and surmounting the obstacles in his way. The stops, the flankers, and the seweller all have their own specialised tasks to perform.

The cameraderie of the beating line is a feature of driven shooting. Beaters usually notice everything, especially the performance of the Guns, and are renowned for their pithy comments both on marksmanship and safety. It is a pity more Guns don't have their own back when the beaters have their shooting day.

While beating a straight line must be maintained, or pheasants will run back through any kink. It is obviously easier to control a line in a game crop than in a thick wood.

146

Pickers-up

Pickers-up, too, come from all backgrounds but share the common interest in gundog work. It is one of the areas of shooting which also attracts the active participation of women. On most driven days there will be two or three teams of retrievers or spaniels with a handler usually positioned well back behind the line of Guns. Their main task is to retrieve dead and wounded birds which fly on before subsequently falling. They, too, see all and are in a better position than most Guns to know what has actually been hit.

At the end of the drive the retrieve is achieved in a sandwich movement, the Gun in the middle. While the Gun will start retrieving those birds near him he may be joined by the pickers-up on one side and the beaters with their dogs on the other. It is usually accomplished quickly and efficiently, although if a wounded bird has not been picked a team may stay while the others move off to the next drive.

William Drew, with Tern, well laden after a drive from Piked Acre to Cats Gallows on the Downham Estate.

Tony Hudson, having killed the cock pheasant, has his cartridges replaced by his attendant. This practice considerably increases fire-power but should not be undertaken without the permission of the host.

The Loader

Prince Bernhard of the Netherlands always prefers his loader to be seated.

Many guns go through their game shooting careers without coming into contact with a loader, but those keen shots who go shooting on double gun days will vouch that good teamwork between Gun and loader is absolutely vital.

Good loaders, the diplomats of the shooting field, are born and not made. Although a thorough knowledge of all aspects of game shooting is a pre-requisite, so are other qualities. The loader must expect to take the blame when things go wrong, but seldom the credit when they go right. He must be a Gun's eyes and ears, ever watchful for approaching game, and have nimble fingers and an unflappable temperament regardless of how hectic things become. The loader must also anticipate when his services will be needed. Last, but not least, he must not only be ready with the correct advice if it is needed, but know instinctively whether or not to proffer it.

In times gone by on big shooting parties, Guns tended to bring their own loaders, preferring someone they knew and trusted. Nowadays who provides what is usually a matter of discussion beforehand. Many big shoots expect to provide the loaders, and it is an advantage to a Gun to have someone by his peg who knows both the ground and the form.

Before a drive begins, practise changing guns with your loader: success will depend not just on your marksmanship, but on teamwork, providing you with a loaded gun just when you want it.

That, then, is the team which will provide you with your day's enjoyment. You will quickly recognise who does what. You will also appreciate that although you may think you are a star turn in the day's proceedings you are, in fact, only one of the several skills involved.

Tel Barnacre 2376

BARNACRE CASTLE
BARNACRE
NORTH YORKSHIRE   HG1 2AD

WILLIAM — THIS IS AN EXCELLENT
INVITATION IN EVERY WAY, NOT ONLY
FOR THE OBVIOUS REASON, BUT, UNLIKE
SO MANY, IT TELLS US EXPLICITLY OR
IMPLICITLY ALL WE NEED TO KNOW   EG

5ᵗ November 1988

Would you be able to shoot with us on ①
10ᵗ December? We meet at the Lodge,
ready to move off at 9.15① — and
of course Fiona provides lunch in
the house. ②

① SO OFTEN ONE IS
GIVEN A TIME THAT
MAY BE EITHER
ARRIVE OR MOVE OFF

② ∴ NO PICNIC BUT
TAKE SUITABLE
CLOTHES AND SHOES

③ AND MASSES
OF CARTRIDGES —
AND CASH FOR
THE KEEPER'S TIP !

Knight reports a lot of birds, so
bring two guns③ if you like — but
let me know in good time if you'd
like Knight to get you a loader,
please.

We very much hope you will be able to
make it — and Philippa too, of course.
And by all means bring your funny
spaniels if you like. However, we shall
have plenty of pickers-up if you'd
rather come unencumbered !

Ha ha ! YOUR
GODFATHER IS ALWAYS
RUDE ABOUT THE DOGS.

④ PROBABLY MEANS YOU WILL
BE A WALKING OR BACK GUN — OR ON THE FLANK — SO
START SAVING FOR YOUR
CARTRIDGES NOW !

Your ever,

George.

⑤ MAY BE LATE
HOME.

SEE YOU NEXT W/E

ALL LOVE

D.

7/11/88

PS If William will be back from school
tell him to bring his gun too. Should be
able to give him a bang or two④ and possibly
flight to duck⑤ at close of play.

13

THE GREAT DAY

YOU may be asked to shoot driven grouse, pheasants, partridges, snipe or capercaillie, although you will be very lucky indeed if the last two feature regularly in your diary. Although each takes place in contrasting habitats and provides contrasting sport, the pattern of the day and the organisation needed do not vary all that much. Hence it would probably be best to concentrate on a day's driven pheasant shooting, which is the first taste many Guns have of a driven day.

The Invitation

The invitation may come in good time before the appointed day because many hosts like to arrange their season well in advance, and there is much to organise. Experienced Guns will know that if the invitation comes later rather than sooner it is because another has fallen by the wayside. Someone's loss is your gain. Whatever, much thought will have gone into whether or not you should be asked, and the invitation is not issued lightly. It requires a quick answer on your part.

In accepting the invitation you will need to learn several pieces of information if you are to avoid embarrassment. When should you be there? Is your dog welcome? Is your wife/girlfriend expected? Should you bring your own food? What are you going to shoot? Will you need more than one gun, and if so will a loader be provided? Most hosts will let you know anyway, but if not it is safer to ask than to arrive unprepared.

Keep an eye on the weather. Rain, heavy snow or fog may cause the day to be cancelled. However disappointing this may seem it is no good going to shoot birds which don't want to get up because it is too wet, or which can't see where they're flying if they do. If in doubt ring your host.

This letter of invitation, with its annotations, tells you all you need to know, and a lot more besides.

You may be asked to shoot driven grouse, and if so you will hope for birds and weather enjoyed at Haredon by Michael Collet. The stick marks the safe arc of fire.

OPPOSITE *What to take driven pheasant shooting, with additions if you take your dog (bottom left), and if you go driven grouse shooting (bottom right).*

The Check List

On a shooting day always have a good breakfast. It is surprising how enjoyment, fresh air, exercise or cold will make you feel hungry.

Before setting out, make a check list of what you should take. Many people put two guns in their car in case something goes wrong with one of them. Take plenty of cartridges. It is embarrassing, as well as a sign of your lack of preparation, if you run out. Many people put a case in the back of the car, from which they refill their cartridge bag when necessary. Most cartridge bags will take 50–75 cartridges, which should see you through until you are next near your car.

Your check list should also include what you will need for your dog if you are taking one – lead, whistle, bed, sack, towel, water, and food if you intend to stay on at the end of the day. Take also a length of string, pocket knife (preferably one which has a corkscrew and bottle-opener), priest if you use one, handkerchief, gloves or mittens, handwarmer, scarf and hat, cartridge bag, shooting stick, boots, feet warmers, shooting vest if you wear one, and shooting coat.

If the day involves some walking up, leave the shooting stick and take a cartridge belt. It is always wise to put in some waterproof overtrousers. And of course don't forget your gun and cartridges, which it is quite easy to do. It is as well to take a cloth with which to wipe your gun if it has been raining, and your gun-cleaning kit if you intend to stay.

Under no circumstances take a cordless telephone with you to the covertside. If it doesn't alarm the birds it may annoy your host and fellow Guns, and on some shoots leads to a fine. If you must communicate with the outside world, confine it to a few brief words on your car telephone between drives or during the lunch break, but in a way that it will not delay the smooth running of the day.

You will also need a jacket and some clean and smart shoes if you are going into somebody's house. Alternatively don't forget your rations if you are expected to take them. Some people also include a hip-flask and a bar of chocolate. Take your shotgun certificate (some take only a photo-copy) and your game licence.

Most important, remember money. Try to have £5 and £10 notes as you will need them for tipping. There are special shooting wallets available now, equipped with pads for recording the bag and your shooting appointments and details as well as numbers for drawing pegs, into which you can put your money and certificates. Take your host's telephone number.

The Arrival

Never be late for a shoot. If something outside your control crops up which delays you, telephone your host to warn him. At least he can change his plans and advise you what to do. Try and arrive sufficiently early to give yourself time both to greet your host and fellow Guns, and to prepare yourself. You will be surprised how long it takes you to get into boots and coat and generally gird your loins, so aim to be completely ready at least five minutes before the appointed time because your host will also want you to draw your number and to brief you.

The Draw

Before moving off each Gun will be asked to draw a number and told how many Guns there are. Usually there are between six and ten. Don't forget your number; it will be your peg for the first drive. Each shoot has its own rules about which direction you number from, and how many pegs you move each drive. But unless told otherwise you can assume that pegs number from the right as you face the covert, and you will move two pegs to the left with each drive.

The best pegs are usually those in the centre of the line. With, say, eight Guns out, numbers four and five can expect to be the hot spots and three and six see a fair amount of action too. The higher or lower the number, the less you may expect. When you are one of the last two Guns on the left of the line, you move over to the start of the right on the next drive. Thus the system of moving numbers each drive is the fairest way of ensuring that each Gun has a chance of being at a favourable peg on

There are various devices for drawing peg numbers, and this is among the most exotic. It comprises a piece of silver, containing ten numbered silver bars, engraved with the estate's yearly total. The matchbox gives an impression of its size.

at least half the drives. On some shoots they speed the process up by moving three pegs each drive, but you will be told. You will also be told if, for some good reason, your host wants you to number from the left. It will happen occasionally if a drive is in two parts.

The Briefing

Your host will also take the opportunity to brief you on other matters, such as whether or not he wants ground game or foxes shot. If in doubt, refrain from shooting at either. Your host will want to help his local pack of foxhounds, and he may want his hares kept for the harehounds or the coursers. He may want you to refrain from shooting something special, such as white or golden pheasants. Some shoots tend to regard white pheasants as bad luck and want them shot; on others gamekeepers like them because their absence will signify that something may have gone wrong. Whatever you do don't get it wrong, because you may be in for leg-pulling or even a fine.

Your host may want to preserve his stock of hen pheasants, and may ask you to confine your attentions to cocks only after lunch or at the beginning or end of the season. Even if, on a cocks only day, your host says that you can shoot one hen pheasant if it is a particularly sporting bird, avoid doing so. It is merely his way of

Your host will take the opportunity to brief you.

preventing possible embarrassment should an overkeen Gun subsequently fail to differentiate between the two.

He may also want you not to shoot woodcock, either because he just likes having them around or because he thinks that their numbers are decreasing (in fact they're not; they have increased both in numbers and in range in the last 20 years). But whatever his reasons you must respect his wishes. Under no circumstances question his instructions except for clarification. And if you are in doubt, don't hesitate to ask. Now is your chance.

Your host may want you to refrain from shooting something special. This white grouse was shot at Middlesmoor in 1979 by mistake, the Gun responsible claiming that he was aiming at a bird several yards in front . . .

Going to Your Peg

Then with a 'Guns this way, please' you are off either on foot or vehicle to the first drive. Try not to make unnecessary noise. It is difficult not to talk to anyone else on what is, after all, a social occasion. But keep your voice low and make as little noise as possible the closer you get to a covert; pheasants have good hearing, and more drives are probably spoiled by chattering than anything else.

'Guns this way please.' Moving off for the first drive is an exciting moment.

You may be transported to your peg by vehicle, (although few shoots can boast a purpose-built 20-seater like this converted Army 4-tonne truck); or even by dinghy as shown below at Dillington in Somerset.

Your deportment as well as your dress and marksmanship will be of interest to your fellow Guns. Help others by holding their guns as they get in or out of a vehicle, or over or through an obstacle. You will be shown to your peg by either your host or head 'keeper. Once there don't talk any further, and don't wander over to your neighbouring Gun to coffee-house. Under no circumstances move either yourself or your peg to what you consider to be a better position, or move away from it, unless while placing you your host says that you can. In certain circumstances, especially if you are on the end of the line, your host may say that you can move 'round a bit if you see the birds steaming out over there', but otherwise stay where you have been placed. That is where everybody else, especially the neighbouring and walking Guns and beaters, will expect you to be.

The first thing to do is to assess your surroundings and particularly your field of fire. First you will want to know where your fellow Guns are which, normally, may be obvious. But you may find that the ground is not flat, the line curves, or that there is a hedge between you and your neighbours. Make sure that you know where they are and vice versa.

Second, check to see if there are any stops, or back Guns or pickers-up behind you. Reassure them, too, by lifting your hat or by a wave, that you have seen them. Make sure that you do not shoot at anything coming from or going in their direction.

Third, make sure that you are aware of roads and paths. You may not shoot within 50 feet of a public highway. Make a mental note of telephone or electricity wires and avoid firing at them. Your host won't want uninvited calls from the local electricity board. Your host should also warn you if you are shooting near the edge of his boundary and if there are likely to be problems. Ownership of game is complex: usually it belongs to the owner of the land on which it exists. If you shoot a pheasant and it falls alive on a neighbour's land and you go to retrieve it you may be poaching. If you shoot it dead and it falls on a neighbour's land it remains the property of your host but you may be trespassing if you go and retrieve it!

Leave your cartridge bag by your peg, having ensured that you have enough cartridges in the pocket of your shooting coat to start with. Just check that they are the right gauge – mistakes have been made. Each Gun has his own knack of reloading quickly; there are various ways, but you will have to discover by trial and error which suits you best. Having cartridges in your pocket is handy because it means that you do not have to stoop down to your bag each time you want more.

Your dog should be seated. If on a lead, it should be attached to a peg screwed into the ground. Never attach it to yourself, and remember to take its collar off before it starts work. Place anybody who is accompanying you where it is convenient for you rather than for them – remember that you may need to turn and shoot birds going away behind you.

If you have a companion, it will help you if they make as little noise or unnecessary movement as possible – on one rainy day a businessman asked his chauffeur to hold a brightly-coloured golf umbrella aloft during a drive, and was somewhat surprised to see birds veering off to cross his neighbours. Game birds are no more blind than they are deaf – or stupid. But a companion can be an enormous help as an extra pair of eyes – warning you in a quiet voice, without excitement, of approaching birds you may not have seen.

Adjust your hearing protection and when you are ready, take your gun from its sleeve. It should remain there when you are not shooting, and under no circumstances whatsoever should you ever shoot at anything between drives. If you are using two guns, have a practice or two changing guns with your loader.

Do not load yet. Estimate distances so that you will have a fair idea of what is within range. It sometimes helps to make a mental calculation with the help of some feature like a nearby gate or fence. Have a practice swing or two, but then open your gun, check that there is no obstacle in the barrels, and hold it over your arm with the barrels pointing down. If you should find yourself among others (or crossing a gate or fence) when your gun is unsleeved, always hold it over your arm in the broken position. It shows them that it is unloaded.

Make sure that where you are standing is flat ground, and then either stand quietly, or sit on your shooting stick until the start of the drive. This will be signalled by a blast on a whistle or horn. Now is the time to load.

Loading Up

When you open your gun to load, the barrels will naturally be pointing down. When you close it, make sure that the barrels are still pointing down by bringing the stock up to meet the chamber. If you remember 'wood to metal' it may help. If you do it the other way round you will find that your barrels are parallel to the ground and may well be pointing at your neighbour. The chances of your closing the gun making it fire may be millions to one. No matter, there is still a chance and in any case you don't want to be seen not observing the rules of safety.

When you have loaded, either stand or sit on your shooting stick, your gun underneath your arm with the barrels pointing down, or hold it in front of you with the barrels vertical. Avoid holding your gun diagonally across your chest; the barrels may be pointing only a few inches above your neighbour's head. Keep your fingers well clear of the triggers. Never slip the safety catch off until you have mounted your gun and are about to fire. It is the last thing you should do before squeezing the trigger.

Before you bring your gun onto a bird, try and make sure that there is daylight between it and the top of the covert. Even the dog looks aghast at this Gun's behaviour.

The Drive Begins

The moments before the first birds begin to come over can be fairly tense. Often the odd bird will leave cover immediately and there may then be a lull. Try and avoid shooting any non-game quarry, such as woodpigeon or corvids, before game birds come over, because it will alert them. The only thing you can do is to keep your wits about you; you will probably hear birds coming from a covert before you see them. If you have a companion with you, or a loader, they will also warn you. But at the back of your mind will be three rules: shooting safely, not poaching your neighbour's birds, and identifying your quarry.

The successful Gun is experienced enough to take his time – or make the time – to select his birds and shoot them accurately. For the less experienced marksmanship can sometimes go awry when birds begin to stream over and there are too many to choose from. He becomes flustered, loses his timing and wounds birds. Concentrate on staying calm.

The question of identity is not particularly difficult, unless sometimes on a cocks-only day. But in the tension before the first drive it is surprising how similar, just for a split second, the flight of a starling is to the glide of a partridge. And at least one poor Gun in a woodland rise has shot at a tawny owl, as it flitted out of cover, in mistake for a woodcock (he missed).

OPPOSITE *Double gun drills: The golden rule is always to pass the gun positively with the right hand into the receiver's left and with the safety catch applied.*

161

Before you bring your gun onto a bird, try and make sure that there is daylight between it and the top of the covert from which it has emerged. Quite understandably beaters don't like the sound of pellets rattling through the tops of trees above them, and there is always the chance of an unfortunate ricochet. So leave low-flying pheasants. If one flies towards you do not attempt to make it gain height by shouting or waving your gun at it. That will certainly frighten your neighbour and it won't change the bird's flightline one bit. Much better to ignore it altogether.

The second major point is never to 'swing through the line' (shooting a bird as it intersects the line of Guns). It is bad enough for your neighbour's nervous system to land dead birds at his feet (if you do it means that you are shooting his birds anyway), but not half as bad as staring down the business end of your gun barrels. Be particularly careful about this point when shooting grouse and partridges which generally fly faster and lower than pheasants, thus increasing the risks of an accident.

Try and shoot your birds well in front of you; if you must shoot them going away, for instance in the case of a second bird or second barrel, take your gun from your shoulder as you turn, and raise it again once you have turned through the line. In the case of pheasants, try to shoot them before they set their wings and plane down. This is not always possible, in which case you may have to make allowances for a different angle and trajectory.

If you are shooting ground game, be very careful indeed of your field of fire, and especially so towards the end of a drive when the line of beaters is coming through to the edge of the covert in front of you.

The whole question of which is your bird and which is your neighbour's is vexed, and that you must make a quick decision only adds to the problem. Basically there are four types of birds you will have to consider. The one that is flying directly toward you, or which will cross the line of Guns at a point nearer you than your neighbour is definitely yours. Feel free to shoot it. However there may be an element of doubt if the bird intersects the line exactly between the two of you (and an awful lot seem to). Feel free to shoot it, but if you are concerned that it might have been his, apologise. He will probably do the same to you. If you both fire at it and it falls dead, tell him what a good shot he is. If it is a runner it is probably more polite to say nothing, but do ensure that it is picked.

The main difficulty is the bird which intersects the line at an angle. It may become the concern of three Guns, the one on one side of you as it flies across his field of fire, to you as it flies directly over you, and to the gun on the other side of you who reckons that he can shoot it as it flies behind the line. You need not concern yourself on his behalf. What you have to decide is whether to shoot the bird coming towards you or leave it to the Gun across whose field of fire it is flying. In fact he should leave it to you. It is your bird. The only thing you have to try and work out (as if you did not have enough other things on your mind just at that moment) is a) that it is high enought to shoot, and b) where it is going to cross the line.

Of course you can make a mistake and it happens all the time. If you do, apologise at once if there is an opportunity, or immediately after the drive has finished.

There are always special circumstances, of course. For example a host may ask a good shot who is placed next to a novice to 'help him out a bit', or indeed the novice himself may ask his neighbours to help themselves – after all host, gamekeepers and beaters like to see the results of their efforts in the bag.

The problem is what to do if your neighbour continues to shoot your birds when you are perfectly capable of shooting them yourself. However tempting, try and resist doing the same thing to him. Who knows, by behaving impeccably you may get the message across to him whatever the doubts you may have. However hosts miss little. Yours will quickly realise what is happening, and ensure that an invitation does not go to the offending Gun again. Other Guns – and the chances are that the Gun on the other side of the 'poacher' is also suffering – will also take stock. If you go in for a 'pheasant war' it will also be noticed, and you may also suffer accordingly. Much better to hide your chagrin cheerfully. Things have a habit of evening themselves out on the shooting field.

If you can restrict your thoughts to these three points you will not go far wrong. You can then get on with the actual shooting, and put into practice what you have been taught at shooting school.

Don't move away from your peg for any reason, such as to retrieve a bird, while the drive is in progress. Remember to mark everything you shoot, including those you may have wounded. If a bird flies on but with a leg down it is a sure sign that it has been hit. At the end of the drive, when pickers-up come to help you retrieve, you must be able to give them precise details of what you have not been able to pick yourself. They don't want vague directions, and they certainly don't want to be told that you thought it was a cock and it was dead when it was a hen which has legged it fast into the nearest cover. Your host is on a tight schedule, and the accuracy of your marking will help him stick to it.

Everybody Out

You will hear the advance of the beaters' line through the covert. On some shoots the noise is restricted to the steady tap, tap of beater's stick against tree trunk. On others there is a cacophony, from instructions to dogs, to other beaters, urging birds to flush, or warning Guns that they have.

The end of the drive will be signalled by a blast on a whistle or horn. Unload immediately and under no circumstances shoot anything after it – you may be asked

More or less organised chaos after a partridge drive.

to go home if you do. Put your unloaded gun into its sleeve. Never leave your gun propped up against anything. There is a chance that it will fall over and be damaged. If you have to, lay it flat on the ground.

Retrieve the birds you have shot. Try and give clear instructions for wounded birds which have either flown on or run. If there are doubts about whether you or your neighbour shot a bird, leave it for him to pick. He may be leaving it for you and if so, pick it yourself and indicate to him that you have 'picked his bird' without making too much of a song and dance – there is a point at which politeness can be overdone. If the bird flew on but was hard hit, the matter of whose bird it was becomes secondary to telling the pickers-up about it.

Put any wounded birds out of their misery. Do not avoid this and learn to do it quickly and efficiently. There is nothing worse than struggling Gun and struggling bird and a cloud of feathers. There are three methods. One is a tap on the head with a priest. For those who think that priests are unnecessary, learn to wring its neck, which is quick, clean and efficient. One method is to twist the bird's head once and then pull sharply. Don't overdo it or you will find that the two become separated. A

164

The game cart for grouse needs to be fly-proof. The drawers of this one enable the birds to cool, and the 'keeper to keep each drive's bag separate if needs be.

third method is to bite the bird's neck immediately behind the head and so sever its spine. But do not shirk this unpleasant task; it is your duty to do it.

Treat game with care. Apart from showing respect for your quarry, the carcase is valuable. Go to your local butcher and you may expect to pay £4 for a brace of pheasants (up to £6 plucked and drawn). Although the European market, which is a vital outlet, was swamped with pheasants last season, shoots could still expect to sell their birds for £1.50 a brace, which over the season can help to recoup the costs. For partridges and grouse the returns will be much higher. But with pheasants game dealers can pick and choose, and they won't want badly shot birds, or birds which have been stood on and mangled, are muddy and have just been thrown on a hot heap in the back of a Land-Rover. In any case leaving them in a heap will preserve heat which will affect the speed of decomposition. On many shoots there will be a game cart, or a vehicle equipped with hanging facilities, so that birds can be hung in braces and transported quickly to a cool game room.

At the end of each drive carry your birds by the neck and give them either to the 'keeper or a picker-up. If delivering them to a vehicle, lay them down rather than just dropping them or throwing them in the back.

Try not to waste time at the end of the drive, and don't leave anything behind. Pick up your empty cartridge cases. The modern plastic cases do not disintegrate like the old cardboard ones, and look unsightly. It may also be of personal interest to you to keep track of the ratio of cartridges to kills. But don't raise it as a topic of conversation.

Partridges at Sutton Scotney are hung in a Land Rover.

Rejoin your fellow Guns and make your way back to the vehicles. There may well be points to talk about from the drive, and some leg-pulling, but under no circumstances raise the question of your own performance. You can rest assured that it will have been noticed, and your reputation will not be enhanced if you try and bring it to the attention of others. Your contribution to the bag, or that of other Guns, is never a topic to start discussing, although it is perfectly in order to give or receive compliments about marksmanship.

Between drives try and remember the number of your next peg. Be helpful to other Guns – hold their guns and equipment going over gates, through fences or getting in or out of vehicles. They will also help you – but if you are passing your gun to anyone to hold and it is not in its sleeve, make sure that it is broken.

Walking Gun

On certain occasions during a driven pheasant shoot, most probably when your number is either the first two or last two, you will be asked to be 'walking Gun'. You will join the line of beaters, either in the line or on the flanks of the covert. Your job is to take care of those birds which either fly back, or slip out of the side. You must be especially careful to observe the rules of safety. Concentrate on keeping abreast of the line unless, if you are on the flank, the 'keeper has told you to move a few yards forward of it, in which case maintain the distance as you advance through the covert. Do not shoot birds going forward to the Guns, or ground game, and make sure that you do not swing through the line. In fact being a walking Gun is one of the bonuses of being either a low or high number, and you may well have plenty of sport. You will also see the day from another angle and enjoy some of the comments.

Alternatively you may be asked to stand behind the line of beaters at a certain point in mid-covert as it moves away from you. Again, your role is to shoot pheasants which fly back. This is potentially a time for accidents, partly because you are on your own and there is nobody to take your cue from, and partly because you are not absolutely sure where everybody else is. And because you will not receive the warning you would get if you were a standing Gun, your reactions will have to be just that bit quicker. In these circumstances you must take extreme care. Under no circumstances shoot ground game and confine yourself only to those birds which are flying back and which are high enough to shoot safely.

The Inner Man

As the day progresses you will feel increasingly peckish and the question of food will loom ever larger in your mind. Although you may have a bar of chocolate and your flask, the effects of breakfast are beginning to wear off and you are in need of something more substantial.

On most shoots there are six or possibly seven drives. At the height of the season, it is often not possible to shoot much beyond 3.15 pm. If you have set off at 9.30, your host has a little under six hours to accomplish his plan. The only time of the day when your host can catch up, or spare a bit of time, is that period which has been put aside for refreshments. Lunch is a very important part of the shooting day, and it is not taken lightly. There are various schools of thought, but they mostly divide into two which concern time and substance.

There are two options for when lunch should take place, and each has a bearing on what lunch consists of. One is that there should be a break in the midst of proceedings and that it should be at the normal lunch time, about 1.00 pm, and usually after the fourth drive. It means that hungry Guns can replenish and warm themselves. It also gives Guns who have not been shooting particularly well an opportunity to relax and hope that they will do better in the afternoon drives (it also gives those who have been shooting well an opportunity to relax too much and shoot badly afterwards).

However time will be limited. Hosts will want their Guns ready to move off again at about 2.00 to make the most of the light, but it is surprising how good hospitality in a warm room can dull the Guns' sense of urgency.

The second school of thought shoots through and has lunch after the last drive. There are several benefits. Full advantage is taken of the light. After the last drive Guns can relax in the knowledge that they are not going to be hurried or constrained by the need for full concentration afterwards. Beaters can leave at a reasonable time, gamekeepers can finish their chores, and it gives the birds a chance to settle back into the coverts to roost. If you are 'shooting through' your host will probably arrange for light refreshments – a cup of hot soup and a roll – by the covert side after the third drive to keep the pangs of hunger at bay.

Whichever the choice, the shoot lunch makes special demands on a hostess. For a start, the food required needs to be filling and warming. If lunch is in the middle of the shoot, there will be limited time to eat it. There is no point in her producing a magnificent feast if Guns have to leave it half way through because of the call of the covert side. For that reason it may consist of one main, substantial course – filling stews or steak and kidney pies or puddings are popular – and cheese and fruit. It means that people will have time to eat the main part of the meal without hurrying, but that if the host is behind schedule he can start chivvying over the cheese and fruit stage. Many are the Guns who have departed to the covert munching a piece of cheese on the hoof and with an apple in the pocket (make sure it is not your cartridge pocket).

*Lunch is a very important part of the shooting day,
and in August on the moors there is time to savour
some of Britain's loveliest scenery.*

The time factor may also decide where lunch is eaten. Putting boots and coats on and off takes time, and many shoot lunches take place in stables, barns or outbuildings. Wise hosts make sure that there are adequate loos nearby. Some shoots have their regular lunch rooms equipped with a roaring fire and cooking facilities, but where it is not necessary for the Guns to take more than their coats off. If lunch takes place after the last drive, it may be a far more leisurely and relaxed affair, and it gives the hostess more opportunity to show off her skills. It may also take place in your host's house.

You must come prepared for either eventuality. Put a pair of shoes in the car in case you do go into the house. You can't go in in boots, and it would be embarrassing to wander round in socks especially if you have worn a hole in them. If you do not have a shooting suit, it might be as well to put a sports jacket in as well, although in most cases you can get away with a sweater.

There are three general rules about shooting lunches. One is to beware, especially if lunch is in the middle of the day, of the effects of alchohol. Although it is an affable occasion, shooting and too much drink simply do not mix. A drink or too may do you no harm, but if you become too relaxed you will become careless, and that is the last

*The music room at Sledmere House provides a
sumptuous setting for the pre-lunch drink.*

thing you want to be in charge of a gun. Furthermore, although drink warms you up initially by increasing the rate of your blood flow, by the same action it also disperses your body heat more quickly and you will get colder faster (wildfowlers never take alchohol onto the marsh with them; always a Thermos of soup or something else warm). With a tightening of the laws of gun ownership it is quite possible that sooner or later the police will apply the principle of drink and driving cars to drink and guns. After all, it is your local chief constable who decides whether or not you can own a gun.

The second thing is always to keep an eye on your host so that when he wants you to move off you are ready. The third is to thank your hostess for her trouble. Your host will appreciate it as much as she does. Lastly, try and remember your peg number.

The lunch hut on Peter Duckworth's Bleasdale moor is largely taken up with a rhinoceros head. The brass plate below it reads as follows:

Big Nick

Believed to be the only rhinoceros shot 'in the wild' in the British Isles. Destined for Blackpool Zoo, Bigi Nikki, as he was affectionately known by the Masai children of the Ngora Ngora, was parked in a railway siding at Garstang station on 28 March 1923. He is thought to have been panicked by the passage of the Coronation Scot en route from London to Glasgow at 1.15 am. Breaking from his reinforced container, he made for the hills and was sighted two days later on the Bleasdale Fells.

Cornered and eventually shot at The Arbour by a police marksman from the Lancashire Constabulary using double ball and wad.

1.4.28

For some a quick ziz after lunch is an essential part of the shooting day.

After the Last Drive

After the last drive you will return to your host's house or the meeting point where you may have lunch if you haven't already, he may invite you in for tea or a drink while the bag is sorted out, or you may say your thank-yous and good-byes and disperse. You will have a few minutes to take boots and coat off, to rub your dog down, give it a drink and make sure it is comfortable. If it has been wet, take your gun out of its sleeve and rub it over with paper toweling and then an oily cloth. Make sure that your gun is safely stowed away out of sight.

Before you go, thank the head gamekeeper. It is more than customary to tip him; it is obligatory ! There are no hard and fast rules about the going rate, and very often there is discussion amongst the Guns as to what the agreed amount should be. As a general rule you should not give less than £10–£15, and the same per 100 birds in the bag is about right.

Usually he will be present when your host gives you a brace of birds, often a cock and hen. Many hosts leave that role to the gamekeeper so that the opportunity for you to thank him in the traditional way is provided. On some shoots, however, birds are left on the wing-mirrors of Guns' cars (some have driven off without realising). But the last thing you want to happen is for you to enjoy your host's hospitality only to find on emerging that the gamekeeper is no longer to be seen.

Game books are immensely more interesting if illustrated by photographs and maps.

On some shoots you will be given a game card on which will be recorded the bag and the names of your fellow Guns. From this you will be able to extract the details for your own game book. You can be sure that details of the day will be put into the shoot records. Not only is it for posterity. In this day and age the value of a shoot is estimated from the records, and accurate records are essential. Most hosts usually do them then and there, so that nothing is chanced to memory.

You may be asked in for tea, but unless you have been specifically asked to stay on, do not dally. There is still a lot for your host to do. Take your cue from the other Guns. Thank your host and hostess, say farewell to your fellow Guns, and depart. Don't forget to write to your host afterwards. It is a small effort on your part and he will appreciate it.

Dog Care

When you get home, deal with your dog first. You will know what to do to provide it with adequate food and water, and ensure that it is warm and comfortable. Dogs react in different ways after a hard day's work, but for many the best way to recover is peace and quiet for a long sleep. You will want to check your dog over for any cuts and bruises. You will also want to ensure the following day that there are no muscle sprains which were not obvious the previous night. Anything wrong may become apparent when you take your dog for a walk to get the stiffness out of it.

OPPOSITE Thank-you letters, in whatever form, are vital.

BARNACRE

14 November 1988

I was asked if I'd shoot - through the middle, to boot,
First time over in early November.
So if given the time for this doggerel rhyme
I shall tell of this day to remember.

There's not very much worse when writing in verse
Than to cope with new names that won't scan -
Such as Aspinall (John), Carter, Cross, Wilkinson,
Whose names I'll leave out, if I can.

When John did the draw, he said to me "Lor',
You've picked a real dud, me old son."
But for once he was wrong, for a beautiful throng
Came flying straight over my gun.

The Gate House was good; but, oh, the Big Wood
Where I stood number four on the drive!
The sky went all black as pack after pack
Streamed over like bees to a hive.

John's Labrador, Cass, a round sort of lass,
Brought her birds to John A at the run,
Down, up, through the stream, as fast, it would seem,
As in days when lissome and young.

Lunch sped in a jiffy trying not to get squiffy
On tonic and gin. All a'whirl   Bank
But with nicely filled tank I took post at Spoil/
To be beaten by sun, wind and curl.

Next came Pig Hill and Storeys; but I feel an
De trop in this much laboured rhyme,   more is
Whose object is, host, to send you the most
Special thanks from me, A, of all time.

It really is great to have such a mate,
And despite what I said, I will fully
Stand up 'gainst all comers through winters and summers
For the one that they called the "shoot bully".

A well-equipped gun cleaning area. Note the cork surface of the dresser and walls, and the numerous cleaning rods which avoid frequent changes of heads.

Gun Care

The second thing to turn your attention to is your gun. Modern powders do not affect the barrels in the way the old corrosive ones used to. All the same it may have been raining, your gun is valuable, and you will want to make sure that it is cleaned inside and out as quickly as possible. How you clean your gun is a matter of choice, but to be effective it should be done in two parts, the metal and the wood.

Some people have a baize-covered work surface for this to avoid damage or scratches to the gun. A measure of baize to put over any temporary surface will do as well, but if you haven't got this thick newspaper will do. Remove the fore-end and barrels from the action.

First dry the gun thoroughly. Check also that water has not accumulated in the ribs, and dry them with kitchen paper. If the day has been very wet, it is sometimes worth doing as wildfowlers do to protect their guns from the salt and mud of the marsh. They tend to spray the barrels and action all over with oil to make it lift any residual water. They then thoroughly wipe the excess off so that only a thin film remains.

Remove the surplus dirt from the barrels. Rolled up wads of newspaper, or paper toweling, do this perfectly adequately. If this is not sufficient, use a phosphor-bronze brush on your rod. Push a flannel patch attached to the jag on the end of your rod through the barrel. If it emerges clean you will know that the barrel is too. Reverse it for your other barrel. Then spray the inside of the barrel with a little gun oil, but don't overdo it. If you do not have a spray, put some on the end of a piece of kitchen paper. Then use the woollen mop to remove the surplus, leaving a thin film of oil.

When you have cleaned the barrels make sure that the chambers are clean, for it is surprising how dirt can collect. While you are cleaning the barrels, always check them for dents or other damage. If any, you must take the gun to a gunsmith. Under no circumstances should you continue to shoot with it.

Clean and dry the action, and remove any surplus oil. Make sure that oil does not go through the striker holes. Furthermore do not allow gun oil to spread onto the wood on the stock or fore-end. First remove excess water and mud. Use rolled up tissue paper or pipe cleaners for the nooks and crannies, and pay special attention to the chequering on the grip of the stock and the fore-end.

The wood may have one of five finishes, varnished, lacquered, french polished, oil-finished or even wax finished, and your treatment of the wood will vary accordingly. The gunmaker will supply you with the necessary instructions.

When finished do not put your gun back in the sleeve, which may be damp. Either put it in your gun cabinet, or lock it away in its case in the gun cabinet. At the end of each season it would be as well to take your gun to the gunmaker so that he can strip it down and check it.

Hanging and Drawing Birds

Your next chore is to hang the birds you have been given. Hang them separately and well off ground level out of reach of cats and dogs, away from any source of heat, or variation of temperature. A larder is ideal, or a well-ventilated stable or other outbuilding, or cellar. Some people hang birds by the neck, others by their feet, arguing that by not distending the innards it improves the taste of the meat.

In times gone by, before fresh meat storage was possible, meat tended to be fresh and tough, or strong and tender with spices playing a prominent part in masking bad meat. Game meat has a strong taste; hanging it will bring it out and also make it more tender. The length of time will depend on the size of the bird and the state of the weather.

The shooting season can cover the whole gamut of weather. While you will not need to hang a young grouse shot on a hot August day, you will certainly have to hang an old bird shot on a cold December day for up to a week. If you do not have a room with a constant temperature, you will have to pay close attention to the temperature if the weather changes. The length of time you hang a bird will also depend on its age. For partridge it may vary from three to four days for a young bird in September

A garage is often a good place to hang game. Note the game hooks. A fly-proof sleeve, or some other method of keeping flies away, is essential in warm weather.

weather to double that for an older bird shot later in the season. You can hang older pheasants for up to ten days, woodcock and snipe for no more than three to five days unless it is very cold, and hares up to two weeks. You do not need to draw woodcock or snipe.

If you are not going to pluck and draw the birds yourself, make sure that you have lined somebody up to do it as soon as possible after hanging them. You won't want to find yourself with two ripe birds in search of a plucker. However if you do it yourself it will not take long. Start from the neck down. Do not pull the feathers 'against the grain'. Pull them in the direction in which they hang or you may tear the skin. Remove all feathers from the body, even the small ones. Some people singe the bodies over a candle to remove extraneous matter such as hairs, but make sure that you don't singe the skin.

Before you draw a bird lay out some newspaper, at least three sheets thick. Make a horizontal cut in the vent sufficient for you to insert fingers and pull out heart, lungs and intestines. Try not to make the cut larger than necessary.

Remove the head as close to the breast cavity as possible, pulling the neck skin back towards the body to ensure that it will fold over the cut. Remove wings from the outer joint, and the feet. While removing the feet try also to remove the tendons from the legs. This will not be difficult if you have a set of poultry shears equipped with a semi-circular indent at the base. Cut round the outside of the joint of the leg

176

and foot and pull; the tendons will usually come away with the foot.

Wash the birds inside and out, and dry them with paper toweling. You can either cook the birds immediately, or deep-freeze them. In the latter case put them in separate plastic bags, try and get as much of the excess air out as possible, and seal them tight so that air cannot get in. Don't forget to label what they are, their sex and age, and when they were shot. It is surprising how similar carcases in plastic bags can look. It is wiser to make notes before you do the plucking; birds of a feather look even more similar without them.

Sex and Age

Sexing a pheasant is obvious because of the cock's more colourful plumage, long tail feathers and red wattles around the eyes. Partridges are not so easy, especially if they are redlegs or chukor-redleg hybrids. A redleg cock will have larger spurs than the female, and will be slightly larger and heavier. In the case of grey partridges, the horseshoe mark on the breast of the male will be more noticeable. On adults the crown of the male will be browner, and the female whiter.

Grouse are also not easy because of local variations of colouring. But generally the cock's comb will be redder and larger than that of the hen, and the plumage of the hen may be paler and the bars more distinct.

Some people can tell an older pheasant by the plumage and by the size of the spur. Adult redleg partridges do not have the white tips to their primary feathers, which disappear after the first year. On grouse and grey partridges, examine the outer primary feathers. The older the birds, the more rounded they will be.

But probably a safer way of ageing birds is the presence or otherwise of the bursa, a small hole close to the vent which is present in all young game birds. The older the bird is the more closed the bursa becomes. In adult pheasants it closes altogether.

You may get a day as a Gun at a field trial, as shown here at the trial organised by the Bristol and West Working Gundog Society at Abergavenny.

14

OTHER DAYS

Cocks Only

TOWARDS the end of the pheasant shooting season, and sometimes at the start of it, you may receive an invitation for a 'Cocks Only' day. This is not a men-only party; the object of the exercise is to thin out the cock pheasant population on shoots which depend on the breeding success of wild birds. Cock pheasants are polygamous. If they succeed in establishing a territory they are likely to try and attract a number of hens.

The success of a hen being able to hatch and rear a brood depends on the security and peace and quiet she has. This will not be helped if she is an object of competition among several cocks. Hens may move from one cock to another, but this is different from being harassed by a crowd of them. Game Conservancy research indicates that a cock can manage up to five hens, but that on average it is only two or three in the UK. In America and Eire the ratio has been as much as one cock to ten hens with no drop in fertility.

Therefore safe in the knowledge that they cannot overdo it, shoot managers try and reduce the cock population drastically. Although cocks-only days tend to be more informal – it is an occasion to introduce sons to driven shooting or to give the 'keeper a day – they take the usual format.

As far as you are concerned your problem will be to tell the difference between a cock and a hen, which in the heat of the moment or with the sun in your eyes is not always that easy. Just take your time – darker colouring and length of tail should help you recognise the cock. Your host knows the problems and if you do shoot a hen he'll probably just pull your leg. He may even tell you that you can shoot 'one sporting hen' during the day. Don't take him up on it – all he is doing is avoiding embarrassment for the Gun who makes a mistake.

Snipe

The pattern of the day on a driven shoot does not vary much with each quarry, except possibly for snipe. The surroundings will be different of course, but by and large the rules remain the same. With snipe you will find that there may be up to 15 or 16 drives a day, and you will be moved smartly around a fairly large area of countryside.

The secret with snipe shooting is to find where the birds are, and that depends on sound local intelligence. Your host will have gone to a great deal of trouble to find out. You can pass field after field which might carry snipe but don't until, like magic, the vehicles stop at the one which does. Snipe are very wary, and you will need to be quiet and conceal yourself if the birds are to be driven over you. Instructions will probably be given to you inside the vehicle. Don't slam the door as you get out. Keep as quiet as possible, and a low profile, as you get into position.

Depending on whether or not the snipe are 'in', the drive may consist of a wisp, or hundreds. There will be no pegs, and you will probably find yourself positioned behind a bank or hedge. Do not show yourself. You will have little time to get your shot in. Snipe fly low initially when flushed and then gain height – the hedge behind which you are standing may be the factor that forces them up.

Therefore you may prefer to shoot them going away behind the line. Ensure that your field of fire is safe, and don't fire at a low snipe: the chances are that you will not have had the opportunity to inspect your surroundings thoroughly. Don't despair at your marksmanship. Snipe are notoriously difficult to shoot, and if you are doing better than one bird per seven cartridges you are above average.

Mixed Day

On many smaller and private shoots, where the input is by the members rather than a professional and the emphasis is on quality rather than quantity, there may be a mixture of driving and walking-up game and a mixture of pheasants and partridges. Although such days are usually informal, with family and friends helping with the beating and picking-up, the rules about safety and good manners are never relaxed.

There may be several variations. Some drives may be to all standing Guns, or all Guns will walk-up, or some Guns will join the line of beaters to drive birds over other standing Guns. The difference is important, because you will need to know whether or not you can shoot birds going forward. If you are a walking Gun in a line beating towards standing Guns, the rule is not to.

If you are walking-up game across rough ground or even through a covert when there are no standing Guns in front, you will find yourself placed alternately

Snipe. Very elusive and difficult to shoot. You can expect to bag one bird for every seven shots – if you are shooting well.

When walking up try to keep the line straight – a straight line flushes birds better – and never point your gun down the line.

Shooting snipe, one of the most difficult and elusive of all quarry.

between beaters and, hopefully, dogs. In this way there is a fair chance that all the ground will be covered, and all Guns have an equal chance of something being flushed in front of them. On such shoots there is unlikely to be the abundance of game that there is on a driven shoot, so you must make the most of your opportunities.

If you are used to shooting driven game and birds flying over you, you may find it difficult to adapt. Once you get over the initial surprise of a bird exploding from cover in front of you you must react quickly to get a shot in before the bird has flown out of range. There is some compensation in the fact that the amount of swing you will need, compared to a bird flying over you, may be less. Some Guns also find it difficult to adapt from the faster flying grouse and partridges to pheasants. Only a visit to a shooting school and practice will sort these problems out.

There are important rules. You may find that you are positioned much more closely together than a line of standing Guns. Always try and keep in line and an equal distance between you and your neighbours, for once the line becomes ragged there is a chance of a mishap. Load when the line starts moving. Either carry your gun over your arm with the barrels pointing downwards, or with the barrels vertically in the air. Don't carry your gun at an angle across your body so that it is pointing down your neighbour's ear.

While moving forward keep an eye on whether or not your field of fire is safe should a bird get up – the time you have for a shot is restricted to from when the bird has gained sufficient height for a safe shot to when it is out of range. You may be surprised how short a time that is.

If something is flushed in front of you, and flies directly away from you, it is your bird. If it gets up to one side of you use your judgement, in the split second available, as to whether it is your neighbour's bird or not. If he fires and misses, then feel free to shoot it. Always be careful that the bird has gained sufficient height for a safe shot. Under all circumstances, and particularly in the case of ground game, be very careful that no dogs are in the line of fire. If a bird decides to depart at an angle it may be best, from the safety point of view, to leave it to somebody across whose front it will fly. If a bird decides to fly back – in the direction from which you have come – do not swing through the line. Mount your gun only after you have turned and only after being absolutely sure that a shot will be safe.

When a bird has been shot, the line will stop and will not continue until the bird has been retrieved. While this is taking place, unload and do not reload until the line has reformed and starts moving forward again. At the end of the piece of ground you are walking up, unload and put your gun back in its sleeve until you have arrived at the next cover to walk-up.

On these mixed days don't take a shooting stick. You may want to vary your clothes a bit, because the walking will keep you warmer. You will also want boots which are comfortable to walk in, rather than just decorative and warm. Water-proof leggings will be very useful, especially if you find yourself walking up through beet or kale. You may also want to swap your cartridge bag for a cartridge belt. Some Guns also leave their gun sleeves in the car; others carry them across their shoulders.

The chances are that your dog will be welcome, especially if it is a spaniel or other breed suited to hunting up and flushing game. It will not be so welcome, though, if it hunts so far ahead of the line that the game it puts up is out of range.

Pointers and Setters

Walking up can take two forms. One is what we have just described, with a mixed line of Guns and beaters with dogs which flush the game. The other is over teams of pointers or setters, and a day with these dogs in pursuit of grouse (a traditional way of shooting grouse) is one of the most absorbing sports.

Walking up grouse over English setters. Field trial champion Achelpon Matt of Sharnberry, nearest the camera, backs Jack of Sharnberry. The Gun is William Town.

Beaters are not required. Guns walk in a line, the dogs quartering the ground for the scent of game. In common with most other game birds, grouse will not flush until forced to. Once the pointer or setter has the scent of the bird, it will 'point', standing rigidly with nose pointing in the direction of the bird. It will not move until its handler tells it too, or sends a spaniel in to flush. In that time Guns will have had time to get into range and for the host to have positioned them. Then, and only then, will Guns load up. The word will be given and the bird, or hopefully covey, will be flushed.

You may cover many miles of rough and beautiful country, and you will feel that you deserve every grouse that you shoot. But you will have to dress accordingly. You will need stout leather (or synthetic) boots with thick soles which do not chafe but which support your ankles. Ordinary rubber boots are not advised. A cartridge belt is essential.

You may also not want to carry a heavy coat – the chances are that you won't get cold but you might get wet. One answer is a lightweight rainproof which you can fold up and attach round your waist when not in use. A game bag, or leather thongs for carrying game may also be useful. Take a bar of chocolate because it may be some time before you see food.

SOME SHOOTING TERMS

Like most other pastimes, shooting has its own language. You will pick it up as you go along, but the following may help you in the initial stages.

The male pheasant, partridge, grouse, blackgame, ptarmigan, capercaillie, wigeon or teal is known as a cock, the female a hen. Collectively they are called pheasants and partridges. Grouse, ptarmigan, blackgame, capercaillie, duck, woodcock and snipe are the same, singular or plural.

In the game bag partridges and grouse are counted by the pair, called brace, and even half brace for a single bird. A bag of pheasants is counted by the individual bird, not by the brace, although a pair of pheasants is referred to as a brace. On the other hand woodcock and snipe are counted by the couple.

The bag: Roy Nicholson, head 'keeper at Barnacre, counts the bag. It is wise to lay the bag out in this way, particularly on let or syndicate days, so that Guns can see for themselves what they are paying for.

The beater: A 'keeper will brief his team of beaters and pickers up just as the host briefs his Guns.

The beater: A 'keeper will brief his team of beaters and pickers up just as the host briefs his Guns.

The forward *allowance* (or *lead*) is the space you must aim in front of a crossing or approaching bird to ensure that it flies into your pattern of shot and you shoot it cleanly.

A *back Gun* is one or more Guns set behind the line of Guns on drives when a large number of birds is expected over, or a standing Gun placed behind the line of beaters to shoot birds which fly back.

The *bag* is the head of game, and 'various', which has been shot during the day.

A *beater* is a member of the team whose job it is to flush game over the standing Guns.

To *blank in* is to drive birds from outlying cover to a central covert from where they will be flushed. A *blank drive* is when no birds appear (yes, it does happen).

A *bouquet* is when a large number of pheasants are presented to Guns at the same time.

To *break cover* is when a bird or animal leaves the sanctuary of a covert. A bird which *breaks back* is one which flies back through the line of beaters in the direction from which they have come.

To *brown* is to fire indiscriminately into a covey of partridges or grouse without selecting one to aim at and is considered 'bad form'.

A *cheeper* is a young game bird, which should not be shot at.

A hare is said to *clap* if it stays motionless in the hope that it will not be detected.

To shoot a bird *cleanly* is to kill it instantly, preferably in the head so that the carcase is as undamaged as possible.

A *covert* is a specific area, usually a wood, which holds game. *Cover* is the name given to any vegetation which holds game.

A *covey* is a group of grouse or partridges of family size.

A *coney* (in some places a drummer) is a traditional name for a rabbit. A male is a buck, a female a doe.

A *drive* is when game is driven over you. Normally there will be five or more drives in a day on a pheasant shoot.

A *field trial* is a competition to test the ability of gundogs under normal shooting conditions. A *gundog test* is a test under artifical conditions usually using a dummy or previously killed game.

A large influx of woodcock is known as a *fall*.

A *flanker* is the person at each end of a line of beaters or on the edges of a shoot whose job it is to stop game, especially grouse and partridges, from breaking sideways. A *flanking Gun* is one asked to walk on the end of the line of beaters, usually outside a covert, to account for birds which slip out the sides and fly back rather than towards the Guns. They are usually the Guns numbered highest and lowest for that drive.

To *flight* pigeon or wildfowl is to shoot them as they fly to or from their feeding or roosting points.

To *flush* is to cause a gamebird or animal to take flight or break cover. A flushing

point is a place where, either by topography, sewelling, or some obstacle, birds are more likely to take to their wings.

The cry *'forward'* may be given by a beater when he flushes a bird to warn the Guns that it is on the way over. " 'cock forward'' indicates that a woodcock has been flushed. On some shoots the 'keeper will not allow shouting of this nature.

To shoot a bird *in front* is to shoot it before it has crossed the line of guns. To shoot it behind, or going away, is to shoot it after it has crossed the line of Guns.

A *gun* is a shotgun; a *Gun* is somebody who uses one.

The *hot spot* is a term given to a position on a drive where plenty of birds can be expected.

To *mark* is to note where a dead or wounded bird has fallen.

Before setting out your host will ask you to draw your *number*, which will indicate the peg at which you will stand at the first drive. He will also tell you that you are *numbering* up to so many Guns. Each shoot has its own rules, but you may be asked to move two pegs (occasionally three) on each drive until you reach the end of the line, when you rejoin it at the other end. Which way you move, and the number of places, will become clear at the briefing. The system ensures that each Gun receives a fair share of shooting through the day.

A *nye* is a group of pheasants.

A *pattern* is the spread of shot produced by your gun into which the quarry flies.

A *peg* or *stand* marks where you stand for each drive when you shoot lowland game. Normally it is in the form of a stick which holds a card bearing its number. Shooting grouse you will be shown to a *butt*, which is either a permanent fixture built of stone, earth and heather, or a hurdle or some other temporary form of concealment. A gundog is said to *peg* game if it takes it while it is squatting.

To *pick* a bird is to collect a shot bird at the end of a drive.

A *picker-up* is a gundog handler whose role is to retrieve birds at the end of each drive. Often positioned well behind the line of Guns in order to spot birds which have been wounded but which fly on.

A bird *planes* when, in flight, it ceases to fly and glides down on set wings.

To *point* is when, by its rigid stance, a gundog indicates the presence of a game bird close by.

A *pricked* bird is one which has been hit by pellets but which has not been killed.

A *right and left* is to kill successive birds with both barrels without re-mounting your gun for the second of them.

A *runner* is a bird which, although hit, runs into cover on landing.

Sewelling is strips of either paper, cloth or plastic tied at short regular intervals to a long line, usually binder twine, which when laid through a covert in front of the advancing line of beaters will encourage birds to get up and fly.

A *stop* is a beater who has been strategically positioned to stop birds running out of cover.

To *swing* means to bring your gun to the flight line in front of your quarry before firing. You are said to *poke* if you aim your gun directly at game without swinging with it (and consequently miss).

A bird is said to *tower* when, after it has been hit, it flies high before dropping dead. Usually the result of a lung shot.

Various is the term normally given in the bag to account for anything shot which does not come under the heading of game.

Vermin are those animals or birds, such as stoats, weasels, foxes or corvids, which prey on game.

A *walking Gun* is one who is asked to walk with the line of beaters to account for birds which attempt to fly back rather than forward towards the line of Guns. Often it falls to the Guns with the highest or lowest numbers on that drive. *Walking-up* is when Guns walk in line to flush game.

A *winged* bird is one which has been shot and wounded and is incapable of further flight. Usually it will fall quickly but may then become a runner.

A Gun is said to have *wiped the eye* of another if he or she shoots a bird which another has missed. Sometimes refers to a gundog which picks a bird which another has failed to retrieve.

Sewelling: Sewelling is laid across pheasant coverts to encourage birds to fly where they might otherwise walk or run out the end of the covert.

A stop: A beater, posted at the opposite end of a drive from where his colleagues start, whose job it is to stop pheasants running out by tapping a hedge or fence.

Photographic Acknowledgements

We wish to thank the following for the use of their pictures.

T. Blank 34 (top & centre), 143 (bottom); Graham Cox 56 (bottom), 120, 178; John Darling 66, 137, 182; Robert Dickson 62, 73 (top), 74; Game Conservancy 51, 91, 143 (top right); David Hudson 121 (top), 122 (top & bottom); James Purdey & Sons 76; Robin Williams 73 (bottom), 181 (top).

We are grateful to Charles Nodder of the Game Conservancy, Fiona Firth and Rupert Collens of the Marlborough Bookshop, and Mark Firth of Roxtons Sporting Agency for their help and advice.

With the exception of those mentioned above, all the pictures were taken by Alastair Drew who has asked us to include his own acknowledgements which we reproduce herewith.

I am immensely grateful to the many people who have helped me to produce the photographs for this book. All except two of my pictures were taken between June 88 and March 89.

I am particularly indebted to the following who let me take photographs on their shoots: John Aspinall, Lord Clitheroe, Richard Clarke, Peter Duckworth, Simon Marriot, Nic Van Olden, Val Powell, Jonty Ramsden, Richard Reynolds, The Earl of Swinton, Sir Tatton Sykes, Hugh van Cutsem and The Duke of Westminster.

I am also most grateful for the active support of: Academy Leisure (Aigle Boots), Mark Andreae, The Hon. Richard and Lavinia Beaumont, Nigel Beaumont, Jack Blude, John Charteris, Jim Clarke, Archie Coats, John Cross, my sons (and models) James and William Drew, Joseph Cortese of J C Field & Stream, John Hardbattle, Derek Harrison, John and Sandra Halstead, Leslie Hewett Ltd (Peltor Ear Defenders), Christopher Hindley, David Hudson, Jim Hudson, Peter and Carolyn Humphrey MFH, Richard Kitson, Ben Knight, John Martin, Michael Meggison, Leslie and Geraldine Meggison, Frank Momber MFH, Keith Musto (Musto Clothing), The North East Lancashire Gun Club, Roy Nicholson, Ian Peel, Pieter Quarles van Ufford, Ben Smith, Messrs Swaine Adeney & Brigg, Twenty First Century Antiques, Bettie and William Town, Warren Agricultural Machines, Kenneth Woods and David Yorke.

Over the past year I have frequently cluttered our entire house with cameras, bags, films, tripods, negatives, slides, files, chemicals etc in addition to the normal shooting man's paraphernalia. I have used my daughter Charlotte's dark room equipment. To her and to my wife Philippa, therefore, I extend most sincere thanks for their much needed and appreciated tolerance.

ALASTAIR DREW
Chatburn